Magnificent Corpses

Magnificent Corpses

Searching Through Europe for St. Peter's Head, St. Chiara's Heart, St. Stephen's Hand, and Other Saints' Relics

Anneli Rufus

Marlowe & Company
New York

Published by
Marlowe & Company
841 Broadway, 4th Floor
New York, NY 10003

Rufus, Anneli S.
    Magnificent corpses: searching through Europe for St. Peter's
head, St. Chiara's heart, St. Stephen's hand, and other saints'
relics / Anneli Rufus. — 1. ed
        p. cm.
    Includes bibliographical references.
    ISBN 1-56924-687-4
    1. Relics—Europe. 2. Christian saints—Cult—Europe.
3. Christian saints—Europe Biography. I. Title
BX2333.r84 1999   99-15317
235' .2' 094—dc21   CIP

Manufactured in the United States of America

DESIGNED BY PAULINE NEUWIRTH, NEUWIRTH & ASSOCIATES, INC.

First Edition

For Elaine Laporte, who has faith
And for Fuzzy, who has the key to the Magic Kingdom

▼▼▼▼▼

Contents

▼▼▼▼▼

Contents

▼▼▼▼▼

Contents

▼▼▼▼

Introduction

▼▼▼▼

ALL OVER EUROPE—amid Fiats, hedgerows, and Nutella—corpses are enshrined right where you can see them. Sometimes the entire body is on display, dressed in satin and lace, slippers and a hat. Sometimes amputated limbs rest in a gilded box. Pearls frame a wizened heart. Skulls wearing garlands peer from behind glass. Severed hands jut ceilingward. Small dead girls wear blue satin dresses. Mummies with skin like rawhide gleam faintly in the candlelight; they wear vestments and cowls and wimples.

For the corpses, devotees bring roses. They bring snapshots of themselves and of the ones they love, on whose behalf they pray for miracles. All around the saints' remains they set out scribbled thank-you notes, declaring loyalty, asking for favors.

They believe the flesh retains whatever powers the saints had while alive.

For a traveler like myself, not Catholic and not even Christian, the practice of venerating relics contradicts everything I was taught as a Jewish child. We had no saints, no graven images. Flesh once dead must mesh with earth as soon as possible. The first relic I ever saw, a vial of desiccated blood that I encountered in Spain as a ten-year-old on vacation, aroused me in the same way Halloween did, and *The Twilight Zone*. It is a primal appeal.

After that first glimpse I never could resist relics. Afterward the images of scapulae like saucers, of skulls resting on velvet lingered in my head. Having seen *Psycho* I knew what was said about the kind of person who would keep a corpse around the house.

In our synagogue, the only traces of the dead were metal plaques bolted to the backs of chairs, *In Loving Memory of Melvin Glass*. I wondered what a person had to do to get his or her mortal remains put on display.

On the couch after dinner I would switch back and forth between the latest Nancy Drew mystery and a thick anthology of saints' lives, checked out from the library.

These were extraordinary tales of girls who had their eyes torn out, their breasts slashed off, who sang while being boiled. Some were so young they could have been my sisters. A few of their exploits seemed somewhat suspect. In these books, men and women turned bread into roses. They levitated. They whipped themselves until they bled.

Some pierced their waists with spike-lined belts. Some would not eat for days on end. Some raved. Some stayed in trances from dawn to dusk. Some of them showed their hands and feet punctured, streaming with blood, and said the wounds had come from God.

Some slept in coffins, some on cold stone floors when they could just as easily have had a bed. Some women went to great lengths in preserving their virginity—by growing beards, by tearing out their eyes, by letting their throats be slit.

Some saints worked to convert entire nations, which I thought was unforgivable. Some were hermits. Some had visions of a holy fiancé who climbed down off a cross to give them golden rings.

Best of all, their stories did not end with death. I devoured tales of skeletons that cured the sick. I read breathlessly of corpses which refused to rot. They bled for years, or smelled so sweet they made passersby swoon.

The veneration of corpses, whole or dismembered, is arguably one of Western civilization's grisliest traditions. It is also one of the most enduring, transcending time as well as culture: bodily relics of Confucius, the Buddha, and Mohammed have been enshrined and adored through the millennia.

From its earliest days, Christianity has declared war on paganism. Yet venerating relics is about as primitive as it gets.

SINCE AT LEAST the second century, Christian saints' bodies have been collected, preserved, and adored. By the sixth century, clerics were breaking saints' bodies apart and distributing the pieces among themselves so energetically that Pope Gregory the Great, a future saint himself, begged them to stop. Yet the passion for relics only intensified. Amputated fingers, hands, feet, and even heads went to shrines far and wide so that all could share in the dead saints' glory. Along with actual body parts, other items also counted as relics: saints' clothing, the Virgin Mary's breast milk, slivers of the True Cross.

In Charlemagne's time, no church throughout the Holy Roman Empire could be consecrated that did not house a set number of relics.

In the Middle Ages, relics spawned a continentwide craze. Devotees packed their bags and streamed out of towns and villages, thronging the pilgrimage trails. For most, a journey to see the relics of St. Thomas or St. James offered the only valid excuse for leaving home. A pilgrimage promised romance, adventure, even miracles. In a Europe driven by its fear of sin and hell, such journeys offered absolution.

Some 5,000 pilgrims were recorded entering and leaving Rome every day for a good part of 1350. Cities with major relic shrines—like Spain's Santiago de Compostela—were medieval Disneylands. Crowds jostled for a chance to touch or kiss the reliquaries. Sick and dying pilgrims lay in church aisles, groaning in pain and coughing up sputum. The streets surrounding the churches were packed with minstrels, beggars, and hawkers selling souvenirs by which pilgrims could later boast that they had made the trip. During festivals, the crowds grew so thick and so urgent that pilgrims who stumbled while trying to reach a reliquary were often trampled to death.

You weren't cool if you hadn't hit the pilgrimage trail, as Chaucer's *Canterbury Tales* pilgrims were doing: "the holy blissful martyr for to seek/that had helped them when they were sick."

Along the major routes, inns and taverns sprang up which shaped today's tourist industry. The presence of important relics put certain cities on the map. Cologne might be just a sleepy hamlet today if not for its tomb of the Three Kings.

Introduction

▼▼▼▼▼

Medieval nobles and clerics amassed huge arrays of dead flesh. Emperor Charles V set the pace, and the race was on. Some staged high-risk heists, hiring thieves to steal priceless relics from rivals or to break open sealed tombs. The bones of St. Gregory the Great, the former pope, were purloined from St. Peter's and taken to France. Thieves stole St. Andrew's relics from Constantinople in 1210; the relics are now in southern Italy.

Monks were among the most notorious relic-thieves of all. Nuns, too, were caught stealing.

Counterfeiters thrived. The Crusades yielded shoals of bones that poured onto the market bearing false identification papers and were duly enshrined. Cynics noted the canine appearance of many of these bones. Relics purported to be the same part of the same saint were enshrined in several different places at one time. Each one, like a football team, had loyal fans. France and Constantinople both claimed they had John the Baptist's head.

The frenzy couldn't last. Time brought new ways of worship and new ways of thought. Like other intellectuals of his time, Voltaire derided relics as a "superstition" rooted in "our ages of barbarity," when they appealed to "the vulgar: feudal lords and their imbecile wives, and their brutish vassals."

Others used mallets rather than words. During the Reformation and the French Revolution, great numbers of relics were destroyed, stolen, hidden, or lost. World War II's bombs swallowed even more.

Science, too, has claimed its victims—or its victories, depending on how you look at it. Tests have thrown doubt on the annual liquefactions of St. Januarius's blood in Naples. Relics long hailed as those of Palermo's St. Rosalia, credited with banishing epidemics, have been positively identified as the bones of a goat.

The Church has not officially lowered the status of relics, but their glory days are over.

Still, there are those for whom the craze still burns. In 1993, a pendant containing two tiny splinters scarcely larger than eyelashes—alleged relics of the crucifixion—sold at a Paris auction for 100,000 francs, roughly $18,000. And in 1998 a Pennsylvania man was arrested for smuggling relics out of France. A vial of blood siphoned from the allegedly incorrupt organs of Archbishop Oscar Romero, murdered in El Salvador in 1980, was ceremoniously presented to Pope John Paul in hopes that the dead cleric will be made a saint.

THROUGHOUT EUROPE, HUNDREDS of relics remain in their glass cases and golden boxes. Some languish, ignored. Some are in the middle of famous cathedrals, and tour groups glide past them without a glance while admiring the frescoes.

But in certain churches, mummies lie like well-loved mascots. Rosaries dangle from their sinewy hands. Satin slippers shield toes splayed in a helpless rictus. And it is difficult to find a vacant pew in the Paris chapel where the corpse of St. Catherine Labouré lies with its blue eyes wide open. A steady stream of visitors exchange glances with St. Dominic's skull as it peers from his tomb in Bologna, flanked by an X-ray of his bones.

St. Anthony's tomb in Padua is plastered with snapshots of wrecked cars. They are the remnants of accidents whose survivors believe the dead Anthony saved their lives. Pilgrims line up for a chance to see Anthony's severed tongue, to touch and kiss the glass that shields it.

Today the bodies of 20th-century saints are among the most popular. At a seaside shrine near Rome, teenage girls in sunglasses and sandals kneel before the wax mannequin containing the bones of St. Maria Goretti, who chose to be murdered rather than raped.

Introduction

▼▼▼▼

❖

IN WRITING THIS book I set out to journey among the corpses and severed hands whose stories I have loved since childhood. In the scented silence of their shrines, what could this dead flesh tell me? Like Yorick's skull in *Hamlet*, relics send an ineluctable message. But they carry an added enchantment: that of the peculiar men and women—even children—whose flesh and blood they once were. Relics are saints' calling cards. They link the saints to earlier times and particular places, making them more real. You would not necessarily want to invite some of the saints to your next pool party. But in their lifetimes each created a sensation—so much so that here are their dead bodies, now on display, centuries later.

These are the stories of saints' lives, but also of their deaths, and the curious things that have been done to their corpses. These are tales of autopsy, dismemberment, decapitation, and repeated exhumations.

For me, this was not a pilgrimage in search of miracles themselves, but of what has led thousands to believe they will find miracles.

Many more relics are on display in Europe today than would fit in this book. From a vast array I chose a gallery of oddballs, ecstatics, and dreamers, iconoclasts and victims and hermits, artists and travelers. By revisiting their lives, we probe the passions that drove them: in a different time and place and with strikingly different results, the same forces drive many of us today—saintly and otherwise.

That many of these saints soared to fame because of their preaching, their zealotry, and the number of sinners they are said to have converted is, I believe, almost incidental and largely a result of the milieux in which they lived. Perhaps I shall go to hell for such convictions, but it is true that throughout the Middle Ages and the Renaissance in Europe, religion was practically the sole conduit for public passion, for eccentricity, for magic and art and violence as well. The Crusades were "holy" wars, and Botticelli's beautiful faces are those of angels. I choose to view the saints in these pages as individuals of their own times, whose remarkable talents and in some cases madness transcend the religion through which it was expressed.

Some of them I feel as if I have known all my life, having first read their stories as a child with a bent for the grisly and miraculous. Others I discovered for the first time while researching this book. I thought Gemma Galgani was one of these. Devouring the curious account of her autopsy in a library book last year, I resolved to learn more about this fascinating woman whose name I did not recognize. It was only months later, after returning from Italy, that I happened upon a tattered *Penguin Dictionary of Saints* that I had treasured as a college student. Twenty years ago, I went through that book with a yellow marker, highlighting the names of those who most fascinated me. Now I glanced through it again. And there was Gemma, marked so firmly by that vanished college girl that yellow ink bled through the page.

So Many Maidens

▼▼▼▼▼

ST. URSULA AND THE 11,000 VIRGINS
Basilica of St. Ursula
Cologne, Germany

a GHOST IS IN the hotel. I go out to use the bathroom down the hall and come back to find a large pool of water just outside the door of my room, soaking into the rug. I am sure no one could have been here. I am the only guest staying on this floor. It is the middle of the night. It is not raining and the ceiling is not wet. It looks as if someone has stood here dripping for a long time. Standing silently.

Then afterward there is a chewing sound from underneath my sink. Perhaps a rodent but more probably the ghost, gnawing on something horrible.

The town awakes at seven to the clang of bells—a lingering

9

persistent overlay that keeps sounding like it has ended only to start up again triumphantly in some far corner of the city.

Churches are still Cologne's *raison d'etre*, after nearly a thousand years. Which is odd, in the country where Protestantism was born. Images of the Dom are on souvenirs in store after store: on ashtrays, on nail-clippers, on trick ballpoint pens where you can make the towers stre-e-etch. Sometimes the image is a cartoon, the church anthropomorphized, with little arms and fists and legs.

I wake to clasp my duvet around my body despite the summer heat because something is definitely watching me.

I do not mention the ghost to the hotelier, a Turk who speaks six languages and likes to show off the postcards he receives from guests who have gone back home to Japan, pictures of temple bells and cherry trees and Buddhas. He is busy during breakfast playing a game of *Sorry!* with an African man and a Danish girl. He keeps a series of framed pictures on the stairs showing the city bombed, a flat grid smoking faintly. Just the Dom remains, its black silhouette pointing skyward like a benediction.

After breakfast I find a University of Arizona T-shirt crumpled in the bureau drawer smelling faintly of sweat and leave it there, shutting it in. Ten minutes later I am sure that if I check again, it won't be there. Because this hotel has a ghost.

AT THE EARLY twelfth-century church named after St. Ursula, across the train-tracks from Cologne's huge cathedral, the room with the relics is locked. And the man with the key is curiously reluctant to let me in. At first he just stands there, where I have found him smoking in front of the church, and pretends he does not see. Then he blinks as if he sees but shrugs as if to indicate he cannot hear. At last he makes out he can hear, but laughs at all I say.

Because a woman who is scrubbing the front door with a rag calls him cruel names and derides his behavior, he stamps his feet. At last he stalks inside as if he does not care whether I follow him or not.

The church is empty, sunk in shade this early on a rainy morning. Rebuilt after they were bombed to bits like most of Cologne in the war, these pale walls have a soft sheen like vanilla fudge. The man jingles his key, as if he might just drop it back into his pants pocket and walk away. But then he turns and unlocks the room that holds the relics. It is called the Golden Chamber, and the room is full of skulls. Its walls are paneled not with tiles but with human bones. The biggest ones are bolted to the ceiling, stained with centuries and smoke.

ST. URSULA'S LEGEND is one of Christianity's oldest and, if you like horror films, the most romantic. It is a tale of slaughter. No less than eleven thousand virgin girls are said to have accompanied a princess on a voyage over the sea. Eleven ships echoed with their songs and laughter. They sailed to Rome. From there they turned around heading for home, only to reach Cologne where pagans surrounded the travelers and murdered every last girl in a flurry of severed heads and spouting necks and bloody gowns on the banks of the Rhine.

According to a version of her story that circulated throughout the Middle Ages, Ursula was a third-century British princess whose beauty and brilliance were known far and wide. Her father was a minor king and, like Ursula, a Christian. On the other hand, the king of all England was, like most Britons at that time, a pagan. Knowing of Ursula's charms the sovereign sent some delegates to visit her father. A royal wedding was afoot.

Ursula panicked. Desperate to put off her union with the pagan prince as long as possible, she asked her father for one last favor. He was to let her go on a three-year pilgrimage with ten Christian virgins as company. Each of these ten, and Ursula herself, must have a thousand handmaidens. These must also be virgins and Christian as well. Ursula declared that during those three years her fiancé, left behind in England, was to be baptized as well. She dearly hoped his conversion would show him the virtues of celibacy.

Ursula was so persuasive that her father and the prince both agreed. As her departure date neared, virgins began arriving from far and wide. Britons gathered to watch queues of young girls making their way to the ships.

From England, the ships sailed past a Gaulish port, then past what is now the Netherlands. As they sailed down the Rhine past Cologne, Ursula had a strange dream. An angel was telling her she would die here—not now but later. She kept it to herself.

Onward they sailed. It is difficult to imagine so many girls all in one place at one time: so much long silky hair and so many quarts of menstrual blood. And at that point in history, a party of eleven thousand would easily outnumber the populations of most medium-sized towns.

Basel's bishop joined the girls, who disembarked there and started on foot toward Rome. When they got there, Pope Ciriacus welcomed them warmly. The pope had relations of his own in Britain, and so felt drawn to Ursula. After meeting the party, he too had a strange dream, in which he was told he must sail with Ursula's maidens when they left for home. The voyage would end in disaster, he saw in his dream, but that must not dissuade him.

Like Ursula, he kept his dream a secret.

Ciriacus abruptly resigned and announced that he was casting his lot with the virgins. His departure sparked derision throughout Rome. Shocked that a pope would relinquish everything in order to trail along after a bevy of girls, angry clerics struck his name from the papal registry.

Not all of Rome was Christian. The sight of Ursula's ever-burgeoning entourage filled two pagan nobles in particular with concern. So many baptized maidens, ripe for marriage, were sure to produce a great groundswell of Christian babies. The nobles sent word urgently to the Huns. An unmistakable party was on its way, they warned, and would soon sail past Cologne.

Their stay in Rome over, Ursula and her companions set sail for home.

Meanwhile, back in Britain, her fiancé had become an enthusiastic Christian. Having converted his mother and younger sister as well, the prince now had a vision instructing him to take both women to Cologne where they must all wait for Ursula.

Eleven ships glided along the Rhine. At Cologne, armed Huns streamed down the shore, stopped the ships, and swarmed on board.

SOON THEY HAD beheaded every last passenger save Ursula. Stricken by her beauty, the Huns' leader held back his men and tried to comfort her, saying he was sorry all her friends were dead and that he wanted to marry her. She spurned him and he shot her with an arrow.

One virgin had miraculously managed to hide. She watched in terror the butchering of her traveling companions and then the murder of Ursula herself. All that night the girl lay hidden, still reeling. It irked her that they had all tasted martyrdom while she had not. In the morning she killed herself.

Ursula and her virgins were all canonized. They were assigned a single collective feast day, October 21, with the sole exception of the girl who killed herself. Ursula had gotten her wish. She had escaped her wedding. What with the pilgrims who had joined Ursula's party en route, the pope and bishops, the prince and his family from Britain and their retinues of servants, the death toll is said to have been as large as 26,000.

STANDING IN THE doorway to the Golden Chamber, the sexton demands four Deutschmarks. He hardly moves aside so that I have to brush him as I pass.

Bones flock the walls in geometric bands, zigzags and crosses. Vertebrae scatter like thick white blossoms. Ribs curve gracefully while scapulae jut sharply from the walls like blades. Bones spell out *Ursula* and Latin words. I crane my neck to see the femurs overhead.

Below the bones are rows of shelves. Skulls rest here, wearing small cloth caps like yarmulkes. Some of the skulls are wrapped in red brocade with spaces where their eyes stare through. Coats of arms are embroidered on the brocade: leaves, a crown, a cock.

Also on these shelves, between the skulls, are girl-shaped reliquaries. Partly silver, dozens of them: from the waist up, nearly life-size. These are said to contain relics of Ursula's maidens—though not all eleven thousand—and were installed here in the seventeenth century. No two of their faces, coifs, or dresses are alike. Cut-out rosettes over their hearts show grisly bones inside.

True to the chamber's name, gold shimmers everywhere. Gilt foliage surrounds the shelves on which the reliquaries pose, as if the virgins are attending Girl Scout camp. Gilt columns flank the chamber's altar. On the altar, golden candlesticks surround four arm-shaped reliquaries. Each contains armbones. They all point to a golden statue of St. Ursula, her hands outspread as if to say, *Who knew?*

❖

ONE SCHOOL OF thought holds that the massacre took place in the year 238. Others say the year was 452. Others place the date somewhere in between. Here in Cologne, this church is said to have been built on the site of the slaughter not long after it occurred. Yet stories are also told of an old graveyard that was dug up here during the twelfth century.

In 1155, an abbot named Gerlach began unearthing skeletons from the long-disused burial ground. Because Ursula's legend was so popular, he put out word that these bones were those of the virgins. Some say that in order to bolster his claim, and to make Cologne more popular with pilgrims, Gerlach manufactured nearly 200 false headstones incised with girls' names.

Nearly all of what has ever been written and believed about Ursula and the eleven thousand virgins is based on a Latin inscription on a stone in the choir of this church. Installed by a Roman senator named Clematius no later than the fifth century, the stone bears ten lines of chiseled script. These explain that Clematius, having recently returned from the Orient, feels moved to renovate at his own expense this basilica over the site where some holy virgins were martyred.

Subsequent texts have added a flood of details. One version holds that the virgins did not *plan* a southern pilgrimage but that a providential gale blew their ships toward Rome. Others give the princess's name not as Ursula but as Pinnosa.

Another version concerns a Breton prince who wanted to import Cornish women from across the channel to marry Breton men. The Cornish king sent his own daughter among other well-bred virgins. But then the ships were wrecked, their passengers enslaved or killed.

British hagiographer Sabine Baring-Gould dismisses this, as well as the bulk of Ursula's legends, as absurd. He points out that the Huns never visited Cologne, that there never was a pope called Ciriacus. Ursula, he suggests, is the Christianization of a Teutonic moon-goddess named Hörsel. The goddess, whose name echoes Ursula's, kept company with a thousand maidens. She held dominion over the souls of dead maidens—and she traveled in a boat.

ELEVEN THOUSAND IS an unwieldy sum. Nevertheless by the late ninth century it was firmly accepted that Ursula's party contained that many.

Yet very early texts mention only eleven virgins. In Cologne's coat of arms, eleven flowers allude to the legend—though, arguably, eleven *thousand* of them would hardly fit. Other texts mention five virgins or eight. One completed around the year 850 alludes to "several thousand" (*millia*, in Latin). No reliable historical document of any kind even mentions the story, much less sheds light on its death toll.

A prominent abbreviation in writings about Ursula's tale was "XI. M. V." Scholars argue that these initials were too easily misinterpreted as standing for the Latin *undecim millia virgines*: "eleven thousand virgins." They argue that "XI. M. V." stands in fact for *undecim martyres virgines* —"eleven virgin martyrs."

Which begs the question of how so many bones came to be inside the Golden Chamber, and whose they are.

IN THE CHURCH a black marble casket lies under a detailed life-size sculpture of the prone Ursula. She looks uninjured. The marble slab reads *Sepulchrum Sa. Ursulae*. Two sculpted virgins peer down from a ramp, far overhead. Originally a Romanesque basilica sporting impressive galleries, this church was modeled on Paris's Sainte Chapelle and later saw Gothic additions. Each of its eleven large windows was made to represent another thousand of the virgins.

A cycle of paintings spanning three walls tells the legend.

In one of these paintings, all of which were completed in 1456 by a Cologne artist, the ships are under construction in a boatyard. In another, the virgins embark. White sails billow as Ursula approaches, already topped with a halo like a dinner plate. A white whippet leaps. The girls gaze around at their surroundings. Some stare with what looks like wonder, some with unmistakable apprehension. They wear gowns of blue, yellow, green, and red, with capes. Their long hair flows. Waiting to sail, they crowd the ships.

Other paintings show the progress of their pilgrimage.

But then the girls stand, partly stripped, on deck.

Men clamor onshore.

The last painting shows severed heads, wild streams of blood. Dismembered hands ooze gore. Decapitated corpses are dressed in gowns. A man in green tights clubs a bloody girl who looks already dead. His pose is purposeful, his pointed boots set wide apart. A girl in red, an arrow in her chest, stands upright, soon to drop. A bloody-headed girl attempts to aid a dying friend, her arms outsretched. The city's pointed roofs are mirrored in the men's raised blades.

A disembodied foot, cut at the ankle, drains red blood into a flowered shore. Ursula, wearing a golden crown which will not help her, wears a look of resignation. Her broad white forehead surmounts large pale eyes which bear the last traces of trust. A man in brown is killing virgins with a hoe.

Above the riverbank, girls' souls float airborne.

One killer is walking away. His tights are bicolored, one leg red and one green. He glances back.

A COUPLE ENTERS the church and sits in a front pew. She is wearing a Day-glo orange fake fur miniskirt and white patent-leather platform boots. He has a shaved head and a leather jacket. They sit quietly.

To the left of the high altar a model ship in copper and bronze has a prow forged in the shape of a fantastic bird's head and the name *Ursula*.

IN THE CITY that claims Ursula as its patron saint, this church commemorates mass murder. It makes saints out of the murdered dead, whose holiness is linked directly to the way they died.

Though the number of victims is up for debate, the public likes *eleven thousand*. It rolls right off the tongue. The fact that nearly all its dead are girls gives Ursula's story an added *frisson*: virgins, pierced.

Monastic writers would hardly spell out for us whether or not the girls were also raped. How likely is it that a band of bold and no doubt horny Huns would pass up such a chance? Though unspoken, this likelihood gives the legend a proto-pornographic tang which has surely bolstered its prurient appeal.

SOME OF THE reliquaries evoke girls pressing their palms together as if praying. Some gaze wide-eyed from the shelves, as if they're on a field trip. Some peer out from under heavy eyelids, shy. Some have the kind of pious smugness that invites slaps in the face. One has a large chin like a spade. Another's lips are pink against her pallor. One has flushed plump cheeks and thick mustardy hair that falls in ripples, parted neatly in the middle of her forehead. Several simper. One brunette holds her mouth open, as if unsure whether it is all right to smile. One has aquiline features and enviable cheekbones. Another has a snub nose that shows her nostrils, like a pig's.

Some of them look about to laugh. These are the smiles of girls in slasher movies who are beautiful and doomed and do not know.

From Traverse Afar

▼▼▼▼▼

THE THREE KINGS
The Dom
Cologne, Germany

COLOGNE'S CATHEDRAL SOARS like taffy. Stretched so high into the summer sky it seems itself some kind of covenant, some kind of deal with God since stone could not possibly do this all alone. The *Dom*'s towers reach up 450 feet, its crenellated hulk chiseled with rosettes, points and angels, beasts and hooks.

In front of the Dom, in the crowded square known as the *Domvorplatz*, a heart-shaped mylar balloon slips from a child's hand. Her face crumples slowly as she weeps. Along the railings local boys in big boots toss their hair, its tips bleached lemon yellow. One wears a thick pinky ring and talks urgently into a cell phone. The one beside him jigs back and forth on a skateboard with a hula dancer's grace. He wears a hologram medallion which depicts an eye. Around his upper arm is a tattooed Crown of Thorns.

He pats his pockets for a lighter, clenching a pack of Marlboros between his teeth. The pack pulls his lips into an aghast expression, though he is not. Across the square a mime painted completely white pretends to be a statue, standing absolutely still. He scarcely breathes as children wearing plastic backpacks flick his ankles with their fingernails, poke him with pens and jump to clap their hands before his eyes.

In the late twelfth century, Archbishop Reinald von Dassel acquired from the fallen city of Milan a set of relics said to be those of the Three Magi. Rome's acquisitive Empress Helen, later named a saint for her shopping acumen, purchased these relics during her early fourth-century pilgrimage to the Holy Land. Duly installed in Constantinople, they were later moved—or "translated," as is said of relics—to Milan. After that city fell in 1168, many of its treasured relics were up for grabs.

According to the Book of Matthew, these wise men, aka the Three Kings, followed a star to find the baby Jesus newly born in Bethlehem. After tracing the kings' pursuit of "the star which they had seen in the East," Matthew 2:11 recounts how they "saw the child with Mary his mother," then "fell down and worshiped him." They offered gifts: gold, frankincense, and myrrh. The Bible does not give the kings' names but they have come to be known as Balthazar, Caspar, and Melchior.

Balthazar is often depicted with dark skin, clad like an Egyptian. Some say this "western king" was Ethiopian—a suggestion bolstered by Balthazar's gift to the baby Jesus of myrrh, a fragrant resin found in Africa. Caspar is shown beardless, and is said to have come from Greece. The older Melchior, dubbed the "southern king," is the one who brought gold.

The magi's visit to the manger is celebrated as Epiphany around the world on January 6. Shakespeare, like his fellow Britons, called it Twelfth Night. That date has long brought enthusiastic crowds to Cologne's Dom.

It has been suggested that the kings, if they existed, came from Persia. The word "magi," a plural of "magus," derives from Old Persian. In that tongue it denoted a priest. If Caspar, Melchior, and Balthazar were in fact Zoroastrians—priests of the prophet Zarathustra—then they would have been astronomers, who watched the stars.

AS NEWS OF the archbishop's prize raced across central Europe, a stream of travelers descended on Cologne from all directions. This city was rapidly becoming one of the Middle Ages' prime pilgrimage destinations.

Smiths went to work creating a golden reliquary that remains to this day the Western world's largest. Completed around 1225 and installed in the church amid great celebration, the richly jeweled reliquary was shaped like a house and topped with five shining globes. Worked into its gold sides were images of the apostles, prophets, and scenes including Christ's flagellation and the crucifixion.

Inside the box, wrapped in embroidered cloth, the Magi's bones were not alone. Archbishop von Dassel also brought back from Italy the bones of saints Felix and Narbor, two obscure early martyrs who had established a following in Milan.

Into the reliquary went bits of saints Cosmas and Damian as well. The legend of these two doctors, twin brothers, was already widespread as long ago as the fifth century. The twins were said to have offered their services gratis, and were credited with miracle cures. Their most famous feat was the grafting of a severed leg from a black man's corpse onto a Caucasian amputee, who slept calmly through the surgery.

REALIZING THAT THE relics were swelling the city's popularity, church leaders resolved to erect a cathedral that would house them. Work began in 1248, over the ruins of a Roman temple to Mercury.

Rejecting the stolid Romanesque designs that were currently popular in Germany, planners adopted the new lofty look of French Gothic cathedrals. Just as the golden box housing the Magi surpassed all others, it was decided that the cathedral housing that box must outclass, outweigh, and outshine every church of its time.

Inside, the Dom is as big as a village. Its arched ceiling rises so high—well over a hundred feet—that you must wrench your neck to look at it. Some of its stained-glass windows are fifty-six feet tall. (Chartres's, by comparison, measure thirty-eight feet.) The pale stone of the Dom's vastly long but narrow nave is bathed in the light that rushes through these expanses of glass. Window after window depicts saints, dozens of kings, queens, and coats of arms in blinding gem hues.

One window depicts a man wearing a sapphire gown being crucified upside-down. In another are the Magi, clad in red and purple, adoring the golden-haloed child on Mary's lap. Her knees are swathed in aquamarine. Soaring columns march down the nave, pointing to an enormous choir, the gray stone so symmetrical it seems a trick of mirrors.

ALL THE PEWS are packed. This cathedral is the most crowded I have ever seen. Its aisles are a logjam of tourists raising cameras above their heads to shoot.

The organ sounds like doom.

A Japanese tourist wearing a canvas raincoat poses for a photograph. He stands in a candlelit chapel where a life-size sculpted corpse of Jesus oozes painted blood. Pale sculpted women clamor, grieving, clutching vessels. In their low-cut Renaissance gowns the women's breasts are absolutely spherical, like tennis balls. Blood glides down Jesus's prominent ribs, and down his face. His hand is poised directly on his crotch. The tourist smooths his hair behind his ear for the camera, smiling jauntily.

Five rows of human skulls line a velvet-trimmed set of shelves against the wall. Unlabeled, nameless martyrs, they reside unnoticed in the dark. From far away these shelves look like a fancy spice rack.

Someone passes in the crowd with foul breath.

PILGRIMAGE GROUPS WALK in queues, hoisting banners. *St. Irmgardis.* The fiercest concentration of tourists surrounds the golden reliquary, though now it is more a marvel for how it looks than for what it contains. Shimmering like spun honey, its gold flanks show off their throng of raised figures. Prominent among these are the three wise men. Sleeves and crowns studded with cabochons, they offer vessels containing their gifts in a flurry of garnets and amethysts.

A woman wearing a denim vest stands squinting at the enormous reliquary as if she does not know what it is. A yellow balloon on a ribbon dangles from her hand.

A Taiwanese is using a two-part video camera on which the objects he is filming appear on a small separate screen which he holds in his other hand. Strangers cluster around him, peering at his screen. He does not notice. It is much easier to see the church this way than to walk around and look at it.

The Taiwanese rotates from the waist, capturing vaults and choir, a passing priest. Below his screen, a steady stream of instructions appears: FADE ZOOM. We float along after him like river weeds.

On another stained-glass window, a man lies on his deathbed. A huge plant grows out of his abdomen like a triffid. His hands seem to fumble under his robe as if to say *What's this?*

A British woman reads to her friends about the Dom from a guidebook. *Remained unfinished for centuries. Not completed until 1880. During World War II, Allied bombing flattened 90 percent of the city center though the Dom, struck fourteen times, remained standing in the midst of ruin.*

JUST AS IT was seven hundred years ago, before this cathedral was quite so large and before acid rain stained its stone so dark, the crowd is polyglot. Still, most are Germans. It's not hard to wonder how many of the old pilgrims in vinyl windbreakers are former Nazis come to make amends—here at their nation's largest shrine—with heaven in their final days. Their wives totter beside them wearing polyester pants, pink scalps like seashells gleaming through scant silver pincurls.

A BRITISH WOMAN wearing coral lipstick wrings her hands beside a pew.

"Oh *no*," she wails. "I think we have lost Anna."

Almost Juliet

▼▼▼▼▼

ST. ELIZABETH OF HUNGARY
*Church of St. Elizabeth, Marburg, Germany/
Convent of St. Elizabeth, Vienna, Austria*

IN THE TRAIN between Cologne and Marburg a boy is
walking up and down the aisle at night. Stopping outside
every compartment he shifts his weight from one foot to the
other until the occupants look up from their sausage sandwiches, from their copies of *Stern* with its pictures of women,
and see him. He rocks back and forth with no expression. He
is wearing a red sponge clown nose.

ST. ELIZABETH'S BODY lay for centuries in the gorgeous
church named after her in Marburg—a town which her relics
helped put on the map. The box which held her bones was

church-shaped: gilded silver trimmed in copper, laced with golden filigree and purple cabochons.

Today the church, sporting Gothic towers 300 feet high that dominate the little town, is Protestant. Nevertheless, true to the church's Catholic origins, its stained-glass window shows St. Francis in a radiant blue cowl displaying his stigmata. Altars laud medieval knights and John the Baptist. Coats of arms mark the walls. Elizabeth is pictured everywhere. A fifteenth-century wooden carving replicates the saint's starved waist, cinched by a tight blue belt. Her head looks huge by comparison, her red lips full and pensive and her dark eyes lifted, making her resemble Shirley Partridge about to sing backup on "I Think I Love You."

Born a princess, Elizabeth taught herself to starve while still a child. She forced herself to lie on cold stone floors. She loved her man so much it nearly drove her mad.

ONE SUMMER NIGHT in 1207 a troubador came to serenade a castle in what is now eastern Germany. He told the count— Hermann, the Landgrave of Thuringia—that Gertrude, queen of Hungary, had borne a child that night. This child, the troubador declared, was destined to become a very holy girl. She ought to marry Hermann's eldest son.

The count sent representatives to Hungary, arranging with King Andrew and Queen Gertrude a betrothal for their little girl, Elizabeth.

While still a child of four, Elizabeth left home with a party of delegates sent by her future father-in-law. They brought her cross-country to Thuringia where she first saw the castle where she was to grow up alongside the boy who was her fiancé.

Perched atop a mountain, Wartburg castle was famous for its wealth. In its glorious confines the count surrounded his family and his court with delicacies and finery and continuous entertainment. Lyric poets roamed the halls reciting verse.

Yet in this house Elizabeth—born a princess, bound to be a countess—became devout. The little girl padded to the chapel night and day where she lay flat on the cold floor praying fervently. Scolded by her guardians, she would pretend to play with other children but as soon as no one was looking she ran off to the castle's chapel. Although she could not read she seized the books she found there and stared down at the psalms, page after page.

On New Year's Eve in 1216, the boy to whom Elizabeth was promised died. The count decided that Elizabeth must wed his second son. The plan was sealed.

Soon after, Hermann himself lost his mind and died.

When she did agree to play games with other children at the castle, Elizabeth begged God to let her win. Then she distributed her winnings among the poor who lined up regularly asking for alms at the castle gates. The young girl's piety was getting on the adults' nerves. She already had enemies among the court.

When she eschewed her gowns and chose to dress like a poor woman, the courtiers mocked her. Yet Elizabeth found an unexpected ally in her fiancé, Ludwig. The young man always leaped to her defense. A statesman and soldier, Ludwig had fallen in love. He brought Elizabeth presents from his travels. She would rush out to meet him and he would put his arm around her, giving her the latest souvenir. Once, knowing her tastes, he brought Elizabeth a coral rosary.

Elizabeth's servant later wrote that the future countess was darkly pretty, "perfect in body," and that she spoke softly. Elizabeth's enemies warned Ludwig that she was too fanatical to be a normal bride. They urged him to send her back to Hungary.

He is said to have declared that he'd rather give away a mountain of gold than lose her.

She was fourteen when, at twenty-one, he married her.

Unlike other female saints, she neither resisted marriage nor tried to persuade her husband to join her in a vow of chastity. Nor did she take such vows herself. She'd never known such bliss.

She prayed at all hours and he did not try to stop her. Kneeling by their bed, she prayed while Ludwig held her hand.

They had two children.

Elizabeth and Ludwig vowed to mate for life, like swans. If one of them should die, they swore, the other would stay celibate forever.

Elizabeth wore rags and gave away her husband's money. While he was away on business, she took charge of the castle, emptying its treasury and storehouse to feed the poor. And the poor arrived in ever greater numbers, knowing Elizabeth could not bear to turn them away. When the count came back from abroad, his officials would rush to tell him what Elizabeth had been doing. But Ludwig was glad, saying God would bless her for her charity, that God would bless him too.

As she contemplated the ever-increasing number of beggars making their way to Wartburg, Elizabeth began to worry about the steep path leading up to the castle from the valley below. Nicknamed the "knee-smasher," this rocky trail was too harsh a climb for the sick. So Elizabeth built a hospital at the base of the peak. There she went and washed patients' sores, their feet, their clothes. She fed the ill by hand. She shaved the heads of men so sick they smelled like carrion.

When patients died, the countess used her own bedsheets as shrouds and helped to bury the corpses herself.

At the castle gates she fed hundreds every day.

Yet she herself ate hardly anything but bread. Refusing meals at Ludwig's table, she grew thin. She imposed other strictures on herself. She would not wear the elegant crown befitting her office because she pitied Jesus with his crown of thorns.

They say that one day Elizabeth happened to meet a child with leprosy. Filled with sympathy she brought him to the castle, where she tucked him into her own bed. Someone told Ludwig. His patience at last worn thin, the count ran pelting to the bedroom. There he tore away the blankets but, the story goes, the leper had become the baby Jesus. From the bed the child smiled up at Elizabeth and Ludwig, then disappeared.

Another version of the story has Ludwig tearing away the blankets to reveal Jesus crucified, his outstretched arms bleeding into Elizabeth's sheets.

In June, 1227, Ludwig joined the Fifth Crusade. He set off for Italy, leaving the twenty-year-old Elizabeth pregnant with the couple's third child.

Two months later, Elizabeth received a summons from her mother-in-law. The older woman told her that something had happened to Ludwig in Italy, that it was God's will.

Knowing politics as she did, Elizabeth jumped to the conclusion that her husband had run afoul of some local nobleman and been thrown into jail. She told her mother-in-law that she must pray. God—and Ludwig's own influential friends—would set him free.

But she was wrong. His mother said Ludwig was not in jail at all. He'd caught the plague in Italy and died.

Elizabeth ran screaming through the castle.

They say she raged like a wild beast. "The world is dead," they say she shrieked, "and all its joys."

Weeks after learning of Ludwig's death, Elizabeth left Wartburg. It is not entirely clear why. Some accounts say that she departed the castle of her own accord, wishing to adopt a life of holy poverty. But some say that Ludwig's brother-in-law threw her out, that Elizabeth was banished. Two loyal servants accompanied her when she left, but with two children and an infant in tow the group was homeless. It is said that everyone snubbed Elizabeth, terrified that by sheltering her they would anger the new count who had thrown her out. The same families whom Elizabeth had fed and clothed now rebuffed her. Allegedly she embraced her fate with her customary faith. One of her servants later remembered how Elizabeth, plodding destitute around the village, fell into a mire. But Elizabeth stood up, streaming with sewage, scraped her dress, and laughed.

For a while she and her party lived in a pigsty.

Elizabeth had an uncle who was a bishop. Discovering what had happened, he lodged his niece and her companions in his house. But when she learned that the bishop was planning to find her a new husband, Elizabeth demurred, swearing that she would slice off her nose if it came to that, "so every man shall hate me."

She saw to it that her children were placed in foster homes. Then Elizabeth renounced the world and became a Franciscan nun.

She took as her mentor a well-known priest named Master Conrad. A former crusader and inquisitor, he had made his reputation by trying suspected heretics. Elizabeth's husband had admired him. Before Ludwig's death Elizabeth had prayed with Conrad. Now that she was alone and under his jurisdiction, Conrad took to slapping her. He said he had to break her will.

He sent away her trusted servants, saying they reminded the countess too much of the riches she'd left behind. In their place he employed women who watched Elizabeth like the most vigilant spies and reported on everything she did.

One day she visited some fellow nuns without asking his permission. Conrad beat her with a pole. The marks lasted for weeks.

She is said to have been terrified of him, although she reasoned that she must learn to bend like soft grass in a heavy rain.

Her piety grew even stronger, now rewarding her with mystical experiences. Announcing that she was about to have a vision, she sank to the floor one day and stared up at the sky. She laughed hard for a long time, then she wept.

She longed to beg from door to door, embracing poverty, but Conrad wouldn't let her. So she caught fish which she sold for cash to give the poor. She spun wool to make clothes for the homeless and she nursed the dying. When Elizabeth was twenty-three, she fell ill.

She laughed and prayed the days away in what would be her deathbed.

Her corpse lay on display for three days in a chapel at the local hospital. It is said to have smelled sweet. Birds flocked overhead singing the Regnum Mundi. Mourners calling Elizabeth a saint snipped off bits of her clothes and her hair.

IN 1539, THREE hundred years after Elizabeth's death, Count Philip of Hesse raided the church where her body was enshrined. The count, a Protestant, demanded that the monks surrender their saint's bones. Stuffing them in a sack, he rode away with them. He had also stolen a golden cup and crown which Emperor Frederick II had given the church when Elizabeth's relics were formally installed there centuries before. Philip dispersed the relics, hoping they would never be found again. He was Elizabeth's own descendant.

Just as he had hoped, pilgrimages soon came to an end in little Marburg, once nearly as popular as St. James's shrine in Spain.

Some of Elizabeth's relics were never found. Church officials at Marburg attest that part of the saint's remains lie buried here today in a pilgrims' graveyard. Various bits purported to be souvenirs from Philip's stolen trove have turned up in the succeeding centuries all over Germany and France. The golden cup surfaced in Sweden.

Elizabeth's skull and a few of her bones turned up in Austria, where Vienna's Convent of St. Elizabeth enshrined them in a gold-and-glass case. Her skull wears the stolen gold crown.

VIENNA WAVERS IN a heatwave haze as if viewed through a pair of pantyhose. Sightseers scuttle slowly from the massive archways of the Hofberg across hot pavement to Stephansdom. They throw their heads back, balking at an architecture built too large for human habitation. It is a landscape for leviathans. A Hapsburg palace looms forbiddingly, guarding its two thousand rooms. Another one across the city has over a thousand more. A single theater sprawls for half a mile. Its shadow lies across a boulevard wide as a river.

In this blazing heat, on the steps of a cathedral, twenty men and women dressed identically as Mozart pose in buckled shoes and blazers. They are selling concert tickets. Under frothy wigs sweat slides down their cheeks.

Through the hot streets I search for the Convent of St. Elizabeth. In a city of churches, nobody I ask has ever heard of it. Some insist that it does not exist. Finally I find it in the shadow of a hospital—of course. Elizabeth is now the patron saint of hospitals, as well as of nurses, bakers, beggars, brides, and countesses. She is the patron too of dying children, exiles, hobos, homeless people, lacemakers, and widows.

But the convent's iron-banded door is firmly locked. I knock. I buzz a doorbell. No one comes. I go away and come back in the evening. No one answers.

A woman in the parish office says the church is almost never opened to the public. Anyway the head is displayed only one day out of every year: November 19, Elizabeth's feast day. It is a largely private observance, and it's months away. And anyway, *is* it her head?

Poor scattered princess. All we know is that she died in Marburg.

HER RELICS WERE first entombed in a stone monument at Marburg's hospital chapel. This miraculously oozed, they say, a fragrant oil. Conrad, who had beaten her, promptly began the proceedings that would lead to her canonization. Pilgrims testified to miracles.

In one of these stories, a girl was believed to have swallowed the devil in a drink. Her belly swelled grotesquely. Possessed, she thrashed and raved for two years until someone took her to Elizabeth's tomb. There she shrank to her normal size and, it is said, regained her senses instantly.

Elizabeth was made a saint four years after her death. That year, the cornerstone was laid in Marburg for a church devoted specially to her. It would be swiftly built by Teutonic knights.

By that time, Conrad had been murdered.

In 1236, the saint's relics were removed from their original grave as Emperor Frederick watched. Installed in a gilded, jeweled reliquary, the remains were given a place of honor in the new church, and became even more popular than before.

❖

THE JEWELED BOX that held her bones is empty now. It's there, but empty. You must buy a ticket to see it, as you would to enter a museum. The girl who sells me my ticket is a Protestant. She giggles and shrugs when I ask where Elizabeth's bones went.

"I know a man," she says vaguely, "who knows about those things."

In a chapel in the church Elizabeth's reliquary rests, but caged behind a grille that rises to the ceiling interlaced with wrought-iron flowers. Sunshine filters through a window, bathing the gold box in an explosive light. Over 100 of the box's original 800 gems were prised off in 1810 by order of the government. Yet still it glows with amethysts and inlaid rosettes made of semiprecious stones. Carnelians as big as half-dollars frame scenes from her life, crafted in gold: Elizabeth cradling a bowl, feeding a bearded man, holding a spoon to his mouth as the poor crowd all around her. The saint offering what looks like fruit to a woman with many children. On one of the reliquary's narrow ends the Virgin holds the baby Jesus, whose gold sleeve hangs empty, someone having swiped his arm. The box is hinged and has a big ominous keyhole. What monk held the key that let her get away?

The chapel is clearly a girl's room. Halfway up the wall, flowers are chiseled in the stone. The pastel windowpanes are shaped and colored like handfuls of cocktail marshmallows. The flowered floor tiles glow. Wrought-iron unicorns stare from the grille.

Philip, a convert who destroyed his forebear's shrine, was nicknamed "the Magnanimous." He gave Marburg its university.

I stay a long time with the empty box but no one else

comes in. Perhaps this is because you have to buy a ticket. Or maybe it is that she has ebbed from here, her presence vanished with her bones. *Elvis has left the building.*

Throwing specks of color on the church floor, a stained-glass window shows Elizabeth bidding her husband farewell as he sets off for his crusade. The next shows her learning of his death. Her eyes are wild. Another window shows her washing a sick man's feet. Another shows her dying.

WITH LUDWIG, SHE knew happiness. For centuries he has been informally called Blessed Ludwig, even St. Ludwig, though he never has been canonized. He indulged Elizabeth in everything she did, even applauding her for behavior that would have been eccentric in any age, not least for a castle-dwelling countess in the thirteenth century. Hagiography is rife with stories of female saints whose fiancés and husbands shunned them.

Then again, unlike many married saints she did not make a vow of chastity before her wedding.

Yet throughout her life—even after her death—Elizabeth met remarkable cruelty. Wartburg's courtiers mocked and undermined her. A relative may have banished her. Conrad's sadism is fully documented. Finally her relics were desecrated not by just anyone but by yet another relative.

What made all these people so certain that they could get away with it? Did they imagine that Elizabeth, by eschewing the wealth that was her birthright, abdicated the respect due a princess? When they saw Elizabeth punishing her body, did they conclude that she had no self-esteem? In any case they took advantage, as abusive boyfriends blame the women they abuse.

Clearly someone who willingly gave away not merely the dregs but the best of her wealth is an inspiring role model.

Yet Elizabeth's life and death and their aftermath prove that selflessness is dangerous.

Conrad decided he must break her will—or what was left of will in a young homeless widow who had made a vow of poverty. Philip broke her bones apart, and with them broke the flow of pilgrims to this shrine, a tradition that had flourished for 300 years. Today I find evangelical fliers on a table near the church door. Elizabeth is a mere decoration here. Long hailed as medieval Germany's greatest woman, here where once she lived she is a figment, dispossessed.

Keeping Secrets

▼▼▼▼▼

St. John Nepomuk and St. Adalbert of Prague
St. Vitus's Cathedral and St. George's Basilica
Prague, Czech Republic

aT Holosevice Station a Japanese woman eating a pink ice cream and dazed with heat walks headfirst into a pole.

"*Ai,*" she cries as her fat son holding a carryall that says *Who's My Animal Club* stares at her, blinking. A hot spell is sweeping the European plain.

"Europe wilts," reads the *Herald Tribune*, which makes it all sound sad and lovely, like a lily.

Crowds of tourists, mostly young, roam Prague's station with their eyes alight. It is a pilgrims' pride. It is not relics that lured them here but rumors of a city yet unseen: medieval towers rising all around a silver river. Golden beer, and slim Czech girls, each one a Sleeping Beauty, seeking English lessons. In one recent year alone, seventy million tourists went to Prague.

Throughout the station, neon *Wechsel* signs flash even in the light of day. They buzz with savage urgency. The clerks in booths below sit bathed in reddish glare like wallflowers at parties.

Fifteen years ago they all may have been making rugs in factories, pouring cement.

At an agency I arrange to rent a bedroom in a private apartment. I am given a key and told that the landlady's name is Maria. The clerk at the agency studied English with a Cockney. He says, *The ly-y-ydy's ny-y-yme is Maria.*

Maria is not home. I knock, then use my key and go inside and shout Hello, but the apartment remains still. A pair of terry slippers rests atop a mat. A door that separates Maria's bedroom from the rest of the apartment is padlocked. The kitchen has large canisters of salt and sugar, and a bed right next to the stove, prettily made, as if the cook might tire suddenly while stirring mushrooms in a soup.

Four beds are in my room. Their flowered covers hide hard mattresses that might be made of chalk, but gouged. The wardrobe has a pegboard front on which a previous guest has scribbled *Rave!*

The lamp is covered in a shade made from an upturned wicker basket with its bottom snipped away. The shade is singed. I switch the light on and the lamp gives out a cry. The power in the flat goes out.

SIX-HUNDRED-YEAR-old Charles Bridge spans the Vltava. The bridge is packed with walkers shuffling back and forth over the river from the Old Town to the western shore and back. Westward rises the battlemented hill on which Prague's castle broods. Under a blazing sun the hill has palaces, museums, and, on little Golden Lane, Franz Kafka's former home.

Spray-painted on a wall with photographic precision along the street climbing the hillside is a stencil of a sumo wrestler.

St. Vitus's cathedral, the castle district's Gothic centerpiece, took six hundred years to build. Now it is crammed with tourists from around the world. Seeking refuge from the heat they swarm around the shadowed hulk of its interior. Having reached the city about which everyone is talking, they gloat.

"I'm on Salt Lake City time, still," chirps a boy wearing a BYU T-shirt when I ask the time. He taps his watch.

Waving small flags on sticks, the tour guides talk in French, German, and Japanese. Clots of tourists trail behind like fish-spawn. Near the holy-water font a woman puts her hands around her mouth and calls into the crowded gloom, "Shoshana!"

Wenceslaus IV was a fourteenth-century king of Bohemia. Not the tenth-century saint who was the Christmas carol's "good king" Wenceslaus, this one instead was noted for his rage. In 1383, he decided to start seizing church property—a plan that drew protest from religious leaders, including a Prague priest named John Nepomuk. Wenceslaus had Nepomuk arrested, jailed, tortured, and then released. But the priest emerged from jail so severely injured it was clear he would not survive.

Wenceslaus ordered his men to bind and gag the dying cleric. At the king's command, they bundled Nepomuk into a sack and threw it off the Charles Bridge late at night. But when Nepomuk's corpse washed ashore the next morning, everyone knew that Wenceslaus was the murderer. Soon enough he was deposed.

That's one version of the story.

In the other, Wenceslaus was certain that his wife had a

lover. As a practicing Christian, Queen Sophia attended church regularly, where Nepomuk was her priest. Wenceslaus seized Nepomuk, demanding that he reveal everything the queen had divulged in the confessional about her affair. Nepomuk would not speak.

Wenceslaus ordered his men to singe the captive with hot irons. Still Nepomuk remained silent. Finally the furious king had Nepomuk thrown into the river. As he drowned, a ring of gold stars is said to have shimmered over his head.

His relics lay entombed but mostly ignored for nearly three centuries. In 1715, when his name came up for sainthood, the body was exhumed. Witnesses reported their surprise at seeing a fresh, pink tongue lolling in the dry skull. The very tongue said to have kept a queen's secrets now "pulsed with life," one witness wrote.

Canonized in 1729, Nepomuk went on to be cherished as Prague's very own saint. Czechs treasured him for standing fast against a despot. To this day, a cross and five metal stars mark the place on the bridge over which he was thrown.

As for that story featuring Queen Sophia, the Vatican officially declared it false in 1961. Some Jesuits, it was believed, had made it up.

IT COSTS NOTHING to see the rear portion of this cathedral, the swarming darkness near the door. But if you want to pass the altar and see Nepomuk's relics on its right, you have to buy a ticket from young men who stand beside a guardrope.

Under a crimson canopy that sweeps down from the ceiling, Nepomuk's casket catches all the light. Sculpted from 3,700 pounds of solid silver, it soars like a meringue. A silver sculpture of Nepomuk crouches in front. With a long sensitive jaw, the saint looks like Abraham Lincoln. He cradles a crucifix, gazing down tenderly at Jesus. Golden stars spangle his head. Around him, silver angels loll on silver clouds. Some bear huge candlesticks that curve like shofars. Soldier angels wield a broken column. One holds out a torch, and wears a sun medallion on a chain around his neck as if he's posing for an Ohio Players album cover.

High up and only visible from one side, an angel holds what could pass for a waiter's tray. With his other hand the angel points to the tray. Mounted in its center is Nepomuk's alleged tongue. Through binoculars, the strawberry ice cream-pink oval looks like porcelain. A whitish line bisects it. While some accounts claim this is the actual tongue, others say it is a painted vessel with the real tongue stuffed inside.

"There's his tongue," says an American girl with a stud through her chin. She sits Indian-style in a pew, pointing from her guidebook to the angel.

"Yeah, it's tongue-shaped," says the friend beside her, wearing shades.

ACROSS A COURTYARD, tour groups shuffle up and down the nave of St. George's Basilica like husbands waiting for their wives during a sale.

In a small chapel, dark and ominous paintings surround a marble altar. Behind an oblong window near the base of the altar is a skull, St. Adalbert of Prague's. It wears a flower garland, faded blues and white.

Around the skull, a knobbly jumble of bones has been arranged with casual abandon, and draped with dainty chains. A slender armbone lies alone in front, apart from the rest, and bound at both ends with pale pink ribbons tied into jaunty bows. Dried blooms lie scattered on the bones.

The chapel has no candles, no bouquets.

As Prague's bishop in the mid-tenth century, Adalbert devoted himself to converting the city's stubborn pagans.

One of them launched a sneak attack in which nearly everyone in Adalbert's family was murdered.

Adalbert fled. Among the pagan Poles and Magyars he baptized whomever he could. Among his prize converts was the Hungarian leader Géza and his son, Stephen, who would later become Hungary's patron saint. Fashioning himself God's soldier, Adalbert composed war songs in several different languages.

But he lost his war. Somewhere near Königsberg in 997, a pagan priest stabbed him to death.

Poland's King Boleslav I demanded that the pagans relinquish Adalbert's remains. Still furious at the missionizing priest, they held his corpse for ransom, asking Boleslav for its weight in gold. The Christian king complied. Recovering the corpse, he took it home to Gniessen. There it was enshrined.

Soon pilgrims began calling Adalbert's relics miraculous. When these rumors reached Prague, local clerics started insisting that the corpse belonged in *their* city. After all, Adalbert had been *their* bishop.

Gniessen flatly refused. So in 1039, Adalbert's relics were seized by force and carried to Prague.

A FRENCH TOUR guide summons his group, which trails into Adalbert's chapel slowly. Their sweating faces gaze up, tired, at the art. Over the altar, sculpted cupids smile. They show their teeth like evil dolls planning to come alive as soon as they are left alone. Wreathed in its girlish garland, Adalbert's skull stares out through its pane. But it is near the floor, and no one seems to see. Adalbert was worth more dead then alive, though now even that value has dropped considerably.

Take No Prisoners

▼▼▼▼

ST. STEPHEN OF HUNGARY
St. Stephen's Basilica
Budapest, Hungary

i AM WATCHING television in my Hungarian hotel, which is a set of rooms the landlord has jerryrigged atop his family home. The hotel overlooks the highway. Trucks roar past, spewing exhaust, en route to Budapest some twenty miles away. The show is an historical drama. Dark good-looking Magyars gallop back and forth across the sweeping plains and hills around Lake Balaton. A shaman wearing antlers strapped to his head has a vision. Firelight flashes on his spastic face. Men standing in a circle slash their wrists to spout blood into a bowl from which they all drink, one by one. A couple makes love, naked, in a lake.

This small town changed its streets' names in the 1990s. *Lenin út* and *Marx ter* are no more. But no new maps are printed yet which show the current names, so when somebody gives directions it is all, *Turn left after three blocks, go straight until the station.* Like an actor memorizing lines I thread my way through quiet lanes where peppers, winegrapes, and tomatoes gleam on trellises.

On the commuter train to Budapest—a Russian train with *Don't lean out the window* in Cyrillic—passengers are coughing phlegmily. It is a summer hack; everyone has it. Between all the seats the rubber armrests have been picked away by countless fingernails, baring the steel bars underneath. Thin scum is left, the rubber gouged with tiny scallop shapes. It is what captives do. The vinyl seat sticks to my legs, the windows flecked with murdered insects and the toilet calligraphed with diarrhea.

I ride through a city called God.

KELETI STATION THROBS with hotel hawkers. Faces round, noses upturned, they look like hedgehogs. They ask, *Do you need a room in Budapessshhht?* Smut swirls up from the tracks. A kiosk bears a big sign, *Szupermarket*, and a small one, *Do NOT touch the Fruit.*

A man whose body ends at his hips rides a wooden board on wheels, his empty trouser legs neatly rolled up and clipped. His hands, stuffed inside wooden clogs, clack on the floor. His face is somber and smart. Another man, hooting with teeth all black, sits on a folded blanket, showing passersby his puppies in exchange for cash.

A moneychanger sips espresso from a cup no bigger than a walnut, with a tiny spoon. Graffiti on the escalator stair reads *FUX* and *Love, Attila*. On the Metro car someone has scribbled *What the hell has happened?*

Everyone agrees that Hungarians spring from different stock than other Europeans. They don't *look* like their neighbors, and their Magyar language—which contains sounds totally nonexistent in English—is unrelated to every other tongue on earth besides Estonian and Finnish. One school of thought places the Magyars' roots in Han-Dynasty China, where as a nomadic tribe they ran afoul of an emperor who forced them westward and away.

In any case 1,100 years ago they were fierce warriors who swept across Europe on horseback, seizing slaves and terrifying everyone. Under Prince Árpád, leader of the most powerful among the Magyar hordes, they swarmed into what is now Hungary, subjugating towns right and left.

UNDER A NEO-Renaissance dome, St. Stephen's basilica sprawls huge, with seating for nearly 9,000. A sign reads *Silenzio, prego* as if only Italians are prone to making noise in churches. Pointing to the milky skylight and the angels painted on the dome, tour leaders drone in French and German. Sightseeing Hungarians snap pictures of the stained glass. Young girls wearing tube tops giggle at the angels.

ÁRPÁD'S GREAT-GRANDSON, Prince Géza, was lured by the new religion that St. Adalbert of Prague was hawking throughout the territory. In 985, Géza had Adalbert baptize his entire family. The prince's young son, Vajk, dedicated himself to the Virgin and renamed himself István, Hungarian for Stephen—after the early saint who was martyred in Jerusalem. By 995 Stephen had married Gisela, sister of the future St. Henry the Second.

Géza died in 997, leaving open the Hungarian throne. Stephen's elder cousin Koppány claimed it, following traditional Árpád succession rules. Stephen responded by battling his cousin at Veszprem, on a headland north of Lake Balaton. Stephen won. Adopting the take-no-prisoners attitude that would mark his entire career, he ordered Koppány's execution. Ordinary death was too good for a pagan, Stephen declared, and had his cousin cut into four pieces.

To solidify his leadership over the Magyar tribes and to ensure that Hungary would be Christian, Stephen appealed to the pope. Sylvester II sent him a crown and granted him the right to call himself the "Apostolic King."

He got to work. Soon Hungarian soil, long pagan, was sprouting abbeys like so many wild mushrooms. Stephen launched missionaries across his realm. At least one in every ten towns, he decreed, must have a church—and only church towns were allowed to have markets. He announced that the kingdom was under the Virgin's protection. Anyone caught skipping Sunday services, he declared, must be thrashed or killed.

He instituted tithing. He established a law by which those caught stealing would have their hands hacked off. He let his wealthy subjects keep their slaves, yet is lauded to this day for freeing his own.

They say Stephen loved to go out in disguise and give money, anonymously, to beggars. One time he was in the middle of such a foray when, they say, a gang of street people jumped him. Knocking Stephen to the ground they proceeded to beat him, tearing at his hair and beard and seizing his purse. Throughout this assault the king never revealed his identity. They say he merely lay like an insect and prayed to the Virgin, telling her that if his assailants had been pagans he could kill them. But he reasoned that as they were Christians he must suffer this ordeal gladly, and vowed to be even more generous from then on.

Within two decades of his coronation Hungary, formerly

a feared barbarian territory, had become so orderly and Christian that an official pilgrimage route to the Holy Land was posted through it. The tribes dissolved, their old faiths melting.

THIS IS THE summer in which eastern girls dress up like prostitutes. They climb up Castle Hill in satin hot pants, silver tube tops, platforms powder-blue with six-inch soles. And yet their faces do not match their clothes. They don't smile knowingly or smirk but gaze around exhilarated from the joy of shopping.

The train station has a row of kiosks selling panties with lace plackets, sherbet green and Orange Crush and shiny gold. Leopard-spot bustiers. White vinyl bras with fringe.

Two girls are chatting on the Metro wearing chocolate satin flares so skintight you could slide a card between their buttocks. It's not that they don't look pretty, only shocking. They don't know.

The ambulances sweep through town, a constant scream.

STEPHEN'S LIFE-SIZE statue poses underneath the dome in his cathedral, crowned with a sparkling halo, framed with marble columns. Tomorrow, August 20, is his own national holiday. It is neither the anniversary of his birth nor of his death, the usual markers that saints' days celebrate. It is the date of the "translation," when his relics were brought here. Fleshy-petaled flowers cluster around the statue, the red and white blooms with their green leaves mirroring Hungary's flag.

The angels are all pink with swirls of lavender.

This church is a monument to forced conversion.

While Hungarians cherish their stories of shamans and Árpád, and their pagan heritage as a people who came from far away, they also cherish Stephen. And it was he who crushed that vanished world which still enchants them. Almost singlehandedly, like a conquistador in his own land, Stephen bullied his people into changing their entire way of life, body and soul—with no choice and no looking back.

HE HAD BEEN dead forty-five years when, in 1083, Stephen's body was exhumed. This was part of the canonization proceedings that would make him a saint. Witnesses at the exhumation reported that the king was a skeleton— except his right hand, which was perfectly preserved.

One story goes that someone decided to sever the hand then and there. No sooner was the attempt made than a mysterious pinkish fluid started welling up in the casket, obscuring the hand. Everyone bailed it out by the bucketful, but the fluid kept rising.

Another story suggests that not only Stephen's hand but his entire body was well-preserved. After detaching the hand, a nobleman called Lord Mérk took it away and enshrined it in a village whose name was promptly changed to *Szentjobb*, meaning "holy right"—a nickname the hand carries to this day. Later the relic was taken from there and moved from one city to another, hailed as a valuable relic and a powerful symbol, pointing the way to Hungary's destiny.

Turkish forces trounced the Hungarian army in 1526, making Hungary the rope in a fierce tug-of-war between Turkey's own allies and the Hapsburgs. At this point the hand was spirited away to Bosnia for safekeeping. It was not brought home again until 1771.

THE HAND THAT built Hungary is now a fist no bigger than a child's. Occupying its own roomy chapel in the basilica, it lies looking very much like broiled chicken in a clear glass tube mounted on golden feet with claws. Snapped off below the wrist, it is the country's most cherished relic. A golden band wraps around it, studded with bright red jewels like drops of blood.

The steps leading up to the pedestal holding the reliquary are sheathed in a red Oriental rug on which somebody has left a jar of baby's breath. Two men stand gazing, clutching motorcycle helmets to their chests.

A group files in. A Chinese woman sips a soy drink from a box. The guide drops coins into a slot to make a bulb illuminate the hand. But no one on the tour is listening to the guide. They shuffle past the pedestal while staring at the stained-glass windows.

One window shows Stephen's son, St. Emeric. Stephen groomed him for the throne but in 1031 the young prince died while hunting bears. Sainted, he became the namesake of Amerigo Vespucci.

Another window shows St. Margaret, a princess who refused to marry the king of Bohemia, joining a convent instead.

In the main window Stephen himself frowns, his beard flowing down a regal robe comprising panes in many colors.

MY "HOTEL" IS up a set of wooden stairs whose bannister is not firmly attached and swings under my hand. The bathroom door is glass; you have to fill the room with steam to hide yourself. The shower has an air bubble under its floor which bangs like gunshots when I step on it. The landlord watches sports on TV downstairs in his underwear.

In tonight's episode, young Árpád yearns to lead the Magyars.

THE HOLIDAY BEGINS with armed men marching.

Military parades and brass bands fill the streets as the

morning unfurls. Mounted Hussars, cavalry with swords, clatter as flags snap in the hot diffident wind. Folk dancers leap across big wooden stages erected for this purpose near the castle. Two bridges have been closed to traffic in order to accommodate fashion shows and blues bands. Budapest's finest majorettes compete for prizes. Nearly every shop in town is closed. I cannot buy a bottle of shampoo.

Late in the afternoon, a mass is held in the basilica. Crowds start collecting all around the building, men and women in Sunday suits ambling closer and closer to the barricades and TV sound trucks. The sun dips behind blocks of flats; the day's sweltering heat ebbs like a punctured blister. Couples push baby carriages festooned with Hungarian flags. Two little boys duel each other with fat plastic swords in the national colors. Old women in net scarves finger rosaries. Throughout the crowd faces and figures look similar, the dark slick hair and hedgehog snouts, large breasts. Girls wearing tube tops ride their boyfriends' shoulders, waving instamatics, snapping pictures as the head of the parade emerges from the church. The satin banners are appliquéd with pictures of the saint. Crosses are raised high.

A father and son wearing matching jerseys striped red, white, and green stand up on tiptoe, holding hands.

Religious confraternaties march past slowly as dreams, hoisting their flags, chanting *Maria*. Applause ripples through the packed streets as one group carries a doll-like madonna. Squadrons file past holding swords. These days one-fifth of all Hungarians are Calvinists. This country has one of the world's highest abortion rates and ranks second worldwide in suicides.

Alongside me a woman wears a plaited lanyard shaped into a cross. A man darts through the crowd selling paper flags which flick against the sound of drumbeats, *poom*. A camera crew has commandeered a crane and swings out over us, scattering pigeons which swoop near our heads, murmuring. A commentator's voice drones from the steps of the basilica, narrating the parade in tones half soccer match and half ecclesiastical. Choir music swells through loudspeakers. The air begins to smell like diapers.

A woman lifts her small son up and he attempts to kiss her on the lips, wriggling in her arms and thrusting at her.

As the music intensifies the man in the striped jersey blows his nose. Tears glisten on his jowls. Then all around others are crying too, standing quite still.

Hailed now as "Good King Stephen" and "Stephen the Great," it was this saint who made Hungary a nation. His legal and administrative codes withstood the centuries. He regulated ownership of private property, established rules of inheritance, encouraged agriculture, and founded an army. During his reign Hungary's first coins went into circulation.

Under the Hapsburgs and then the Nazis and for decades after, Hungary's national identity has been intertwined with those of other countries. All that Stephen had worked so hard and so ruthlessly to create was subsumed into systems whose rules had been established far away. But after 1989's bloodless revolution, a surge of independence made way for the country's first free elections in 1990 and the last Soviet troops' departure in 1991. As Hungary's patriotism swells apace, so does its love for Stephen, on whose firmly drawn path the country again sets itself. The pagan Magyars are forever fodder for TV.

The priests are bringing out the hand. Amidst wild music and applause it will be walked around the neighborhood, to the Danube, and back to the church, a solemn circuit called a *körmenet* which takes place every year on this day and on Easter. This is Hungary's version of July Fourth and a massive pilgrimage rolled into one. The communists outlawed it.

During those years, August 20 was called "Constitution Day" and "Festival of the New Bread." Completely secular, it banished Stephen from the picture altogether.

Now a roar goes through the streets, the relic with its red jewels jouncing in the dusk. A beating sound comes from the sky. Heads turn. A paraglider kicks his heels, his sails red, white, and green.

Crawling from the Wreckage

▼▼▼▼

St. Anthony of Padua
Basilica of St. Anthony
Padua, Italy

P ADUA'S DOWNTOWN IS under construction. Buildings
swathed in plastic sheeting rise like bandaged limbs.
Below, the city swarms with Fiats revving in the streets and
shoppers seeking lunch. After the blockish boulevards of lower
Budapest, Italy's orange porticoes evoke a dollhouse. Children
freed from school run home to meals of aromatic tripe. They
twirl their candy-colored vinyl bookbags as they clatter down
the colonnades. The straps make whirring sounds.

I HAVE BEEN led to believe that somewhere in this city, in a
certain church of St. Peter, a woman's skeleton lies dressed in

a Benedictine habit. For two hundred years after her death, her flesh remained intact but after the seventeenth century, I have heard, only her bones were left.

Blessed Eustochia of Padua, not quite a saint but partway there, was born in 1444. Her mother was a nun.

Her father took the child to live with him. But his wife and other children loathed her. Eustochia was sent back to live with her disgraced mother, who was still in the convent.

Eustochia begged to take the veil. At first the nuns refused, holding her out-of-wedlock birth against her. But then they relented.

As a young nun, she had violent fits during which she was said to be possessed. Suspicious locals accused her of witchcraft, even of going so far as to poison her abbess. Eustochia struggled to clear her name.

Upon her death at twenty-five, it is said that her corpse smelled sweet. A spring issued from her burial place, it was said, whose water worked miracles.

But Padua's church of St. Peter is not where I have reason to believe it ought to be. Shop clerks in the neighborhood have never heard of it. A woman selling lipsticks and bath oils says lots of churches in the town were torn down after World War II.

"Maybe it's gone," she says, and offers me a free sample of herbal bath oil in a tube.

She laughs. "But Anthony's still here."

HE IS.

The square outside St. Anthony's Basilica is lined with hawkers selling souvenirs out of the backs of vans. His little figure stands patiently submerged in balls of liquid which, shaken, send drifts of artificial snow and glitter over his cowled shoulders. Holding a lily or the baby Jesus, he is depicted over and over again on laminated bookmarks, tape measures, keychains, and combs. In special ball-point pens his figure can be made to glide up and down. You could have a whole set of school supplies in an Anthony theme, or else outfit your bathroom sink. Some vendors sell pink plaster Anthonies which can predict the rain, changing to blue.

IN THE LARGE medieval basilica, after his lunch hour, a priest unlocks the chapel housing St. Anthony's tongue, jawbone, and vocal cords. A line forms at once. It is a long line, snaking backward from the apse. A group of Indian women wearing colorful saris is stealthily sharing a package of Rolos.

The chapel contains a small set of steps leading to a glass window set into the wall. Behind the glass, as in the world's largest china cabinet, shelves reaching nearly to the ceiling are stocked with a priceless collection of vials and jeweled monstrances containing assorted relics. Anthony's are merely the most popular.

Waiting their turn to mount the steps, the Indians quietly pop chocolates into their mouths. Their husbands stand in line beside them wearing drip-dry shirts.

When my turn comes to pass Anthony's relics, I see up close the rime of fingerprints across the glass. In a shimmering and delicate reliquary is Anthony's tongue.

Hewn from a man who died in 1231, the pulpy lobe behind an oval crystal pane is speckled black and pink. Were you to find it on the roadside you might think it was a small exotic cactus.

ONE DAY AT the beginning of the thirteenth century, a strange party of visitors arrived at the Portuguese monastery where a fifteen-year-old heir named Ferdinand was studying to become a monk. Barefoot and wearing rags, these visitors carried five corpses.

The visitors were Franciscan brothers. Their mentor, Francis of Assisi, had fled his wealthy family not long before. Breaking up with his fiancée, the future St. Clare, in order to "wed," as he said, "Lady Poverty," Francis dreamed of converting the Moors. He had made a fruitless journey to Egypt, then sent five of his friars abroad to try again.

In 1219, these five left Italy. In Seville they ran afoul of the Moors, who controlled Spain at that time and imprisoned them, then released them and drove them out of the country. When the five reached Morocco, they preached in the streets. For slandering the prophet Mohammed, they were seized, beaten, and beheaded. Some say the sultan himself dealt the death-blows.

IT WAS THE bodies of these five—now known as saints Berard, Otho, Peter, Accursio, and Aiuto—which the barefoot travelers were bringing home for burial. Marveling over the mutilated corpses, young Ferdinand listened rapt to their bloody tale. He longed to become a Franciscan, in order to be martyred himself as soon as possible.

With the Franciscan habit he took a new name, Anthony. Soon he was en route to Morocco.

He fell ill as soon as he reached North Africa. Unable even to walk outdoors, he lay in bed through an entire winter. Realizing that Anthony had proven a total failure as a foreign missionary, the Franciscans summoned him home. In the spring of 1221 he boarded a ship bound for Portugal.

It foundered in a storm and went ashore in Italy.

Mingling with the brothers at an Italian monastery where he came to live, Anthony was a kind of nobody. Others saw him as a sickly foreigner too feeble to even perform his share of kitchen chores.

Seeking the comfort of solitude, he moved to a mountain retreat. Here he lived like a hermit and seldom left

But one day he was summoned to attend an ordination ceremony. As the event got under way, it was discovered that no one had been assigned to deliver a speech. The superiors went from monk to monk appealing for a volunteer. Everyone demurred. Anthony refused as well. But as the superiors had run out of other options by this time, he was ordered to take the floor.

Hesitant, Anthony began to mumble. His fumblings made the listeners flinch, but soon he gained momentum. In a strong voice he ad-libbed a speech whose fluid complexity held his audience rapt, revealing years of silent scholarship in which Anthony had memorized book after book No one who heard him could believe that this was the same laconic Portuguese who was too weak to wash dishes.

His reputation as a preacher blossomed overnight. Stores would close for the day when Anthony arrived in town, so that every last clerk might go to hear him speak.

THEY SAY HE could appear in two places at one time.

They say he could make a starving horse kneel to revere consecrated bread and wine, ignoring its own oats.

They say that one day while in France, a churchgoer offered to serve Anthony and his companion a meal. The hostess poured wine for both, forgetting to reseal the wine-barrel. Wine gushed out all over. In the hubbub, Anthony's companion dropped his glass, smashing it to bits. Anthony prayed, and the barrel refilled instantly with wine. Scattered shards leaped together to reassemble the glass.

They say that a priest once walked in on him and found Anthony embracing the baby Jesus.

ANOTHER STORY TELLS how a young man once confessed to Anthony that he had just kicked his own mother. Anthony replied that people who did such things should have their feet hacked off. Chagrined, the young offender hurried home and sliced off his own foot. When Anthony learned of this, he lifted the gory member and reattached it to the guilty man's leg.

They say he could stop the rain in squares where he was preaching, though it poured down on the streets beyond.

TODAY ANTHONY'S RELICS attract what is arguably Europe's largest and most ardent cult following. Thousands of letters arrive at the shrine addressed to him every year. Some days his tomb sees well over a thousand visitors who have come to Padua just for this. Busloads come.

The cathedral's gift shop thrives. Along the aisles, pilgrims stand elbow to elbow piling their shopping-baskets with Anthony light-switch covers and Anthony dashboard magnets and fluorescent Anthonies in molded plastic whose seams cut my fingers.

ON THE COURTYARD, near the gift shop, is a pilgrims' travel agency that arranges trips to Lourdes, Loreto and Fátima.

Inside the basilica, crowds surround Anthony's tomb. His bones are hidden deep within this cliff of cool marble. Pilgrims press their palms to it. They push their heads against the stone and *bump, bump, bump*. Bulletin boards mounted around the tomb are plastered with snapshots, silvery ex-votos, thank-you cards in many languages, and long letters to Anthony on flowered stationery.

One snapshot shows a baby in a crib clutching a stuffed Winnie the Pooh. Another shows a dark-eyed little girl.

"Stella was born 9 May 1994 to everyone's great joy," reads the Italian inscription. "But Stella suffered a tumor. She has been hospitalized many times. . . ."

Photographs of lonely-looking girls are pinned to the felt covering the boards alongside pictures showing the same girls as brides. White lace veils hide their eyeglasses.

Many of the snapshots show mangled cars, the aftermath of accidents. Survivors of the wrecks believe Anthony saved them.

No one is quite sure why Anthony is perhaps the world's most popular saint. No one knows how it happened, how this ordinary cleric-turned-preacher has garnered a following so strong and widespread that it unnerves the Vatican. Part of what worries the Church is the tint of magic that colors devotion to Anthony. Devotees prevail upon him to help them find lost objects, often several times a day—usually car keys but anything from hairpins to legal documents. He is said to help recover stolen items too. He is said to protect travelers: sailors and fishermen and people in cars.

Though Anthony was a dedicated celibate, he is hailed as the "holy matchmaker." Girls pray to him for husbands. Goya recorded an annual Madrid festival held near Anthony's June 13 feast day, where street musicians play while maidens line up in the church to ask the saint to end their solitude. Childless, the saint is summoned regularly to help women conceive—because of his reported brush with the Christ child.

The concensus around the world is that Anthony *works*, that he can be relied upon. In which case he is a very popular saint because he is a very useful saint: because of what he does instead of who he is. His memories of Lisbon, his wishes and dreams pale against tales of marvels. It only follows, though such reasoning seems terribly conceited, that if Anthony could rejoin broken glass and amputated feet for *them*, why not for *me*?

In which case it is difficult to draw the line between devotion and taking advantage. Ever the obedient soul who agreed against his will to give a speech when everyone else refused, Anthony apparently still will not or cannot say no. And his devotees turn to him again and again as they would to a trusty appliance.

NOT THAT THE finding of mates or the saving of lives is a small thing. Picture after picture in Padua shows twisted cars whose destruction the faithful survived. Often the devotee is pictured standing beside the wreckage, or a small photo of his or her face is pasted in the corner. *Per grazia ricevuta*, these photos are captioned. For grace received. Dates are inscribed along the border, often cities where the wrecks occurred. Three in a row are captioned in Hindi, others in an Ethiopian script.

Anthony, like the song says about Oz, is a wizard who will serve.

DEPICTIONS OF HIM as a tender nebbish, however, are inaccurate. Though he was ill in North Africa, Anthony eventually regained enough vim to earn the nickname *Malleus Hereticorum,* Hammer of the Heretics. Through northern Italy and southern France he strove to stamp out the gnostic Cathars and other sects. Stories of miracles abound here as well. In one, Anthony made the sign of the cross to instantly detoxify a dish of poisoned food that some murder-minded heretics had served him.

In another, Anthony was preaching to heretics on the beach. They refused to listen, but Anthony's eloquence charmed the fish. They raised their heads above the waves and listened, glistening.

HISTORY RECORDS THAT Anthony's speeches often led to social change: prisoners were freed, the poor fed, debts absolved, apologies made. He did not shy away from lambasting oppressors, and one story is told of a sermon he gave at a moneylender's funeral. Declaring that the deceased had sunk his heart into his riches, Anthony prompted his listeners to inspect the man's treasury. Among stacks of cash they found a human heart, still warm.

Many of those who flocked to make confession in Padua claimed that Anthony had appeared in their dreams and insisted they confess.

By 1231, crowds dogged the would-be hermit wherever he went. Early that year he fled into the countryside and built a shelter in a walnut tree. In his treehouse he rested. But edema had left him swollen and sore. Not yet forty, he knew he was gravely ill and wished to die in Padua. He died en route—foiled again.

AFTER ANTHONY'S DEATH, devotees claimed they saw him in their dreams. Pope Gregory IX declared him a saint within the year.

Padua's basilica was begun at that time for the express purpose of housing Anthony's relics. In 1263 they would be translated there under the watchful eye of a Franciscan who would later be canonized as St. Bonaventure.

When the vault containing Anthony's remains was opened, witnesses saw a disintegrated corpse. Yet in the midst of dry bone and piles of the dust that had once been tissue, they found what they reported was a fleshy, pulpy, ruddy tongue. Bonaventure seized it with both hands and kissed it.

A MAN WHOSE big belly strains his golf shirt holds up the line as he stands and rubs a leather pouch across the glass behind which stands the tongue. Kissing the pouch he pockets it then rubs a stack of holy cards against the glass, empowering his souvenirs. Perhaps he will distribute them as lesser relics to friends when he gets home.

When Anthony's tomb was reopened in 1350, his jawbone was extracted on the premise that this body part, too, made Anthony eloquent. Now on display in the chapel near the tongue, Anthony's jaw with its long teeth is mounted inside a head-shaped reliquary. The head looks curiously feminine, and is crowned with a vast aureole sporting glistening prongs and studded with sapphires the size of almonds. In place of a face is a convex crystal pane. Behind this, in its correct anatomical position, is the jaw. The effect is completely terrifying.

During yet another tomb opening in 1981, Anthony's vocal cords drew their share of attention. Said to be undecayed, these too were removed and subjected to scientific tests whose results declared the tissue perfectly preserved. Now the dark and wizened lumps languish in a crystal sphere poised atop an open book crafted in solid silver. Golden flames leap from the pages to lick the ball. The whole arrangement looks like merchandise in an occult shop, the sort of place that sells Money Draw oil.

A young man standing in the line speaking Italian wears a T-shirt that says *Fuck Your Show Business*. He holds a stack of holy cards and waits his turn.

A Marked Heart

▼▼▼▼▼

St. Chiara
Augustinian Monastery
Montefalco, Italy

MIDWAY BETWEEN TWO seas, my train rumbles
through Umbria's dry hills. The hills slump into the distance
like squadrons of armadillos. Exhaust pouring in through
open windows makes the passengers sink one after another
into a thick snoring slumber though they try to resist. I twist
my backpack's strap around my wrist so tightly that it bites
into the skin, and hurts so badly that it will not let me sleep
and miss my stop.

Then, from the station at Foligno, a country bus glides into
the hills behind the town. Billboards announce an upcoming
horseback tournament whose contestants wear Renaissance

costumes. Summer rain streaks the far horizon as we roll past a villa whose nameplate announces it as the home of an award-winning entymologist. We hurtle past vineyards and olive groves. From the bus stop outside an isolated gas station, a man climbs onto the bus bleeding heavily from what looks like a boil under his eye.

Behind pale medieval walls, the curving lanes of Montefalco are deserted in the late afternoon. I follow signs, under a sodden sky heavy and dark but warm, like viscera about to burst.

Signs with pert arrows point the way to St. Chiara.

NO LIGHT FILTERS through the church's curtained windows so the place feels sunken, underground. Here and there in the shadows, metal surfaces wink. But just to walk up the center aisle requires feeling my way, flailing for pew after pew like someone struck blind.

Squinting around the church does not reveal the mummy which I have reason to believe is here somewhere. A heavy door behind the altar has a doorbell. After a hard ring the window in the door shunts open, like when Dorothy first arrives at the Emerald City's portal in *The Wizard of Oz*. A black-habited nun peeks through, already yelling.

Her voice resounds across the darkness.

Chiara, I stammer. *Want. See. Chiara.*

The nun scolds on, as if she has mistaken me for someone she has been expecting, someone who has failed to take the garbage out, or spoiled the convent's laundry.

C - h - i - a - r - r - a, I simper, rolling my R.

Ah. She blinks, her voice already raised so that it comes out loud.

Ah si.

She rushes off, her feet slapping away unseen behind the wall. Nothing happens.

I ring again.

The window opens with a clatter and the nun is shouting. I whine weakly. The nun thumps away.

A tiny light flicks on. The patch of floor behind me is bathed in a pinkish light.

The saint has lain beside me all this time.

UNDER AN ALTAR whose bulk had up till now been completely swallowed in darkness, the corpse rests behind glass which is protected by a metal grille. The casket's lid is silver.

Chiara wears a habit and her dessicated head rests on a gold-embroidered satin cushion. A brass hoop effects a halo. The dead face is dark, its flesh peeling and curled. Its closed eyelids resemble flattened grapes. The nose is hooked. A rictus twists the lips, making them look unkind. A rounded chin belies the fact that this body has been dead more than 700 years.

Two golden rings gleam on Chiara's folded hands. One sports a chunky stone. A slack white satin pillow spans her legs. Another supports tiny feet whose rawhide toes curl under. Past the corpse, ranging along the casket's glass rear wall, are crimson curtains.

Kneeling on the marble step affords a better view. But still, no matter what, the corpse is set so that you cannot help but stare straight up its slitted nostrils.

Chiara died at forty. Today some, though not all, of her fingernails look painted orange. In the empty church, in total silence, I am gazing at her taut wrist emerging from a wide black sleeve. A smell of mothballs lingers in the air.

Then something moves.

My blood stops as the drapes behind the casket stir. A single eye is peering through the slot between the drapes. Spectacles glint. The eye meets mine, then stays there, absolutely still.

AFTER ROME IT is shocking to sit in an empty church. If you lived in a tiny town whose main attraction was a mummy, would you come and sit beside it all the time or tire of it early in life? Glass lanterns hang from overhead on chains, unlit. The only brightness comes from the small electric light behind the corpse. A slender vase full of lilies throws its curling shadow on the floor. Flanking the casket are ex-votos, dozens of them mounted on the walls, a clutter of silvery hearts. The steps and the altar are brown marble, the color of thick dried blood.

Over the high altar which is painted palest yellow, a custard hue, a canopy drapes down deep red, its tassels swinging. On the walls throughout the church but mostly sunk in darkness are paintings in an earnest, high-school style, the sort of canvases you find in thrift stores. One shows Chiara with her head aglow. In another, she kneels in the streets of Montefalco with a man in flames above her, Jesus probably. Holy cards and pamphlets on a table in the church, invitations to join groups of pilgrims dedicated to Chiara, depict the saint with downcast eyes, like Stevie Nicks.

TRAVELING THROUGH UMBRIA, the novelist Hermann Hesse happened one spring day upon Montefalco. Remembering that visit, the German would write of a strange sight "that is impressed on my memory. . . . I saw a young woman . . . well-preserved in a glass sarcophagus." Her body had been "perfectly maintained," wrote the author. He was no stranger to spirituality. Among his many works is *Siddhartha*, based on Buddha's life.

"The beautiful corpse," he went on to explain, had been a member of the nobility. The woman whose corpse it was, he mused, had been a product of the era and the place that would produce artists like Botticelli and Filippo Lippi. Her presence was "arcane, a little disquieting."

He did not know her name.

So he did not know the story of the contemplative nun born here in 1268. Chiara was dedicated to meditation on Christ's crucifixion. Its imagery provided endless fascination.

At the town's Augustinian convent, Chiara was elected abbess against her will. Her harsh personal regimen impressed the other nuns. She fasted severely. She punished herself for such infractions as speaking aloud during the convent's "quiet time" by standing in the snow barefoot while saying the "Our Father" 100 times. Believing that her habits approached perfection itself, the other nuns strove to imitate Chiara.

Drawing on her talent for diplomacy, she reconciled longtime enemies. Having no money of her own, she gave the poor her rations of food and medicine. From all over Umbria, a burgeoning number of fans came to ask her advice on every topic.

One day a friar is said to have arrived at the convent in a funk, troubled by a scriptural passage that threatened to undermine his faith. Seeking an audience with Chiara, whom he had never met, he agreed to hear the nuns' confessions first.

As he performed this task, a strange sensation overcame him as he listened to one of the nuns. At the sound of this unseen woman's voice, he felt himself melting with what he later called a heavenly longing. When her confession was complete and she was about to depart, the priest asked her where he might find Sister Chiara.

I am here, said the voice through the grille. *It is I.*

Trembling with the ineffable sense of sweetness that had overtaken him, the priest stood up and walked away without another word. As the story goes, her voice alone repaired his broken faith.

Chiara is said to have been marked with bleeding stigmata, and given to frequent visions. She claimed Jesus had told her he was looking for a proper place to plant his cross. These visions often manifested themselves with excruciating bodily sensations, given Chiara's preoccupation with the crucifixion—she has since been dubbed Chiara of the Cross. She spoke of visitations not only from heaven but also from hell, and of how she battled demons.

As I KNEEL watching the corpse, the church's large doors swing open behind me, letting in the afternoon's wet light. An Italian man and woman with their young twin sons burst in, wearing plastic raincoats over expensive summer clothes. The man is still pushing his car keys into his pants pocket. Crossing herself, which sends the sound of squeaking plastic echoing through the church, the mother strides across the floor. At the sound of the doorbell the window opens and a nun appears. Before she can speak the woman raps out a loud question. The nun nods, then disappears. Her slippers thump away.

A set of wooden shutters pops open suddenly in the wall next to the casket. Until now I had never noticed them. A yolky light pours from within.

The open shutters, resembling those on a playhouse, bare an oval opening barred with a metal lattice. Behind this lies a niche cut into the white plaster of the wall. Peering coolly through the lattice is a lifelike silver bust of Chiara in her habit. Crowned with a spiky aureole, she stares out from under heavy lids. The figure's chest is a hollow cavity, housing a swatch of withered flesh that could pass for a pair of sausage patties. *Il Cuore*, says a sign: The Heart.

One day in 1308, Chiara announced that the crucified Christ was "in my heart." When she died soon afterward, many remembered her remark. Amid a hail of claims calling Chiara a saint, her corpse was cut open.

Witnesses reeled.

Chiara's was strikingly larger than an ordinary heart. Surgeons slit it open to reveal, it was widely reported, images naturally occurring in the tissue. A pale crucifix the size of a thumb was said to have stood out, with a red spot denoting the wound in Christ's side. Another protrusion was hailed as representing a lance. Dark and pointed strips of tissue were identified as representing nails. A ring of spiky outgrowths effected a crown of thorns. Yet another protrusion, said to be harder than the surrounding tissue, evoked the marble column against which Christ was flogged. Yet another recalled the scourge itself, down to the knots in its thongs.

A medieval tourist attraction, the heart drew a constant stream of spectators. The natural allure of relics had vaulted to a new dimension.

The rest of Chiara's corpse was eventually declared incorrupt, as its flesh remained intact over the bones. In addition, her blood is said to have remained liquid long after her death. Chiara was canonized in 1881. Nearly a hundred years later when the body was reexamined, its limbs were declared still flexible.

But the markings on Chiara's heart have not withstood the test of time. Today it looks like any ordinary disembodied organ, cut in two and brown with age. A scissor and a bockin lie nearby. Also inside the niche is another, smaller crystal reliquary holding dried chunks said to be Chiara's gallstones which, extracted soon after her death, are said to symbolize the Holy Trinity.

They look like puppy chow.

THE ITALIAN TWINS glance into the niche and roll their eyes. Scampering up the steps to its left they give the mummy a quick look, then turn away. Sighing, they hurl themselves into a pew. Their sneakers slap the floor to signal their impatience.

"Mamma," one whispers as his mother kneels to pray. It echoes through the empty church. "Come *on*."

Letters to Princes

▼▼▼▼

St. Catherine of Siena
Church of Santa Maria Sopra Minerva
Rome, Italy

two nuns in pale blue habits are struggling to remove
sheets from the clotheslines on their penthouse garden. In this
summer wind the sheets billow around a carved stone Virgin
on a pedestal painted tan to match the house. The nuns dart
back and forth. I wonder if they ever go downstairs or if the
penthouse is their cloister and they never leave it, like two
dozen bald Rapunzels. They hover, plucking at the sheets.

Directly across from the penthouse, my room is in the
apartment of a woman who decorates her walls with pictures
of herself. Framed pastels in the bathroom show her naked,
with pink breasts surging up beneath her long blonde curls.

Snapshots elsewhere show her dancing, eating, gazing moodily. Some show her in a satin wedding dress, standing beside her handsome man whose ramrod pose, under lapels like wings, looks martial.

In the kitchen hangs a horseshoe with her photo pasted in the curve next to a picture of the Virgin.

Traffic keens below. The nuns depart the roof garden, cradling their bundled sheets. The last one pulls shut the sliding-glass door behind her.

ITALY'S SEXISM IS large and loud. It is unlike Iraq's, for instance, where women are absent from the landscape. By contrast, Italian women are watched, worshiped, feared—regarded as the source of laundered shirts and joy, the birth of men and gods.

Men dominate Italy's government; they populate the Vatican. They dispense penances from the confessional. They drive the faster cars. Men create most of the films, design most of the fashions, run the banks.

Yet Italy's patron saint is a woman.

Catherine of Siena was neither a noble nor a scholar. Yet in a time of plague she was a diplomat. In a time of corruption she was asked to stop a war. She was illiterate but still told popes and princes what to do.

Her head is in her hometown. But her headless corpse remains in Rome.

FAT POUTING ANGELS with golden wings mount Catherine's casket. In the church of Santa Maria Sopra Minerva, a prone replica of the saint, carved in wood and painted in lifelike colors, lies behind the casket's golden columns. Strong nose, firm chin, thin pink lips resolute, the statue depicts Catherine dead but smart. A large gold ring gleams on its sculpted hand.

Patrona d'Italia, reads a sign.

In 1383, when Catherine was three years dead, Dominicans decapitated her body and carried the head to Siena.

Today a steady line of Italian tourists kneels and nods before the sarcophagus, but quickly. It is as if visiting their patron saint is a patriotic act, like saluting a flag, vaguely obligatory. Perhaps Catherine's pompous titles put them off. Perhaps her bossiness repels them, even though she's dead.

TO THE LEFT of the tomb is Michelangelo's life-size white marble "Christ with the Cross." The cross was clearly just a prop by which he could create what he loved best: beautiful men. Pietro Urbano completed the statue, whose exquisite thighs evoke that transcendant realm where faith and lust converge. But, looking out of place, a clumsy metal loincloth wraps its hips. The Christ was nude originally. Complete with a full set of marble genitals, it drew enthusiastic crowds. Romans lined up in the church to ogle the figure and kiss its foot. Church officials ordered the loincloth bolted on.

This Christ is still the church's top attraction. So many pilgrims kissed the foot that its toes wore away, making Christ look like a leper. Now a bronze shoe, looking out of place as well, hides the damage.

Nearby, Catherine's prone figure in its casket appears as aloof as Michelangelo's Christ is inviting. Dark-lashed eyes serenely closed, she looks as resigned to solitude as he does to kisses.

CATHERINE BENINCASA WAS born the twenty-third child of a Sienese dyer, circa 1347. Her twin died shortly after. One day when she was six, she had what she believed was a vision of Jesus and saints Peter, Paul, and John. One year later the seven-year-old vowed secretly to consecrate her life to God, swearing to stay a virgin.

In due time, Catherine's mother began preparing her for marriage. Good-looking Catherine with her wealth of golden-brown hair was adorned with jewelry and the latest gowns. Her sense of filial duty exhausted, Catherine declared that she had taken a vow. Her mother talked on about husbands.

Catherine cut off all her hair.

To punish her, Catherine's family resolved to deny her the solitude she craved. The large clan made sure she was never alone. Finally realizing that she would not give in, Catherine's parents gave her what she wanted: a room of her own, a kind of hermitage within their house. In this nine-by-three-foot cell she spent her days alone. She slept not in a bed but on a board and wore a hair shirt, woven of coarse animal hair and meant to irritate the skin. Catherine also wore a belt lined with sharp iron spikes. She used a chain to beat herself three times a day. These penitences paid off in what she would later say were visions.

After spending three years this way, Catherine heard what she thought was a message from God insisting that she rejoin the world—even so far as to engage in current affairs.

Leaving her cell, Catherine began haranguing nonbelievers on the streets of Siena. When ministering to the sick, she chose those with the most repugnant and disfiguring afflictions. At local prisons she preached to the condemned.

She still wore her hair shirt and spiked belt, which put her in constant pain. She trained herself to subsist for long spans on nothing but the wafers she was fed at Communion.

Declaring herself gloriously happy, Catherine attracted a group of devotees. Called the *Caterinati*, this mixed band of rich and poor, young and old tagged along wherever she went. As Catherine's fame increased, she is said to have performed scores of conversions. She was credited with miraculous healings and exorcisms. They say she levitated.

One day in Pisa, Catherine took Communion. Having not eaten in a very long time, she promptly had a vision. Jesus hung on the cross. From his bleeding wounds, vivid scarlet beams of light streamed down to her own wrists and feet. Sensing that Christ was giving her the stigmata, Catherine begged him to plant the wounds where he would, but to render them invisible. As she watched, the beams lost their color.

For the rest of her life she claimed to feel the searing pain of wounds no one could see.

Another time, Catherine had a vision of Jesus and Mary. Clasping Catherine's hand, Mary offered it to Jesus, who slipped a ring on Catherine's finger. After the vision, Catherine claimed she wore it still, that it was gold and had a sparkling stone. She felt it on her finger, this engagement ring which no one else could see. (Centuries hence, a nearly identical vision was claimed by another Italian with the same name: Prato's St. Catherine de' Ricci.)

In yet another vision, Catherine traded hearts with Christ.

SHE LIVED DURING an unsettled time. By 1375, Florence and Perugia were rising up against papal control, assembling armies to fight for their freedom. Bologna, Viterbo, and other cities joined the insurrection. For over seventy years, the popes had lived not at the Vatican but in Avignon, France. From Avignon, Pope Gregory XI sent an urgent appeal to the Florentines. It left them unmoved.

Catherine used her skills and influence to persuade leaders in Siena as well as in Lucca and Pisa not to join the insurgents. Selecting her as an official mediator, Florentine officials sent Catherine to meet the pope in Avignon. She told the pontiff she longed for "nothing but peace." The pair spoke of launching a crusade to distract the restless Italians from civil war. Surely they could all unite for the purpose of slaughtering Moslems.

Catherine implored him to leave France for Rome.

The pope listened intently. But soon Catherine learned that the Florentines had sent her to France on false pretexts. They had no intention of reconciling.

Betrayed by the Florentines, she kept up a steady correspondence with the pope, dictating to her secretaries. At her insistence Gregory left Avignon, ready at last to resettle the papal entourage in Rome. In 1378, still hoping to resolve long-simmering discontent, he asked Catherine to visit Florence on his behalf. She went, only to barely escape an attempt on her life. She sorely regretted this near miss, lamenting her loss of what she called "the red rose of martyrdom." Persistent, she negotiated a tenuous peace—only to learn that the pope had just died.

Not one but two successors were named. Roman cardinals elected Urban VI, while their counterparts in Avignon elected Clement VII. Thus began what is now known as the Great Schism, when western Christianity was divided between two popes. Clement held sway over France, Spain, Scotland, and Naples. England, Flanders, Hungary, and most of northern Italy chose to recognize Urban. Catherine fired off hundreds of letters to kings, cardinals, and princes, begging them to mend the split.

She also dictated the manuscript of a book, the *Dialogue*. Based on what she claimed to have heard while in trance, it takes the form of conversations between a human soul and God and is considered one of the most eloquent works of its time.

God appears cheerless, declaring: "The soul who perfectly hopes in me and serves me with her whole heart and will must necessarily put no hope in herself or in the world."

"To me," God recommends, "she attributes all."

A person can taste eternal life, God promises, when "her own will is dead. It is by that death that she realizes her union with me, and in no other way." Denouncing "the hell of self-will," God speaks of the happy soul who "has let go of and drowned her own will, and when that will is dead there is peace and quiet."

"The dead will," God notes, "feels no pain."

ANYONE WHO HAS lived with anorexia knows firsthand the weird magic it works on the mind and the body. Great bursts of energy make you believe you could run for miles, kick a hole through a wall. It brings on altered states, and a conviction that you aren't like anybody else: that you are separate, special, gifted. That your austere ways will make you strong, marked with unearthly beauty. That withstanding hunger equips you for any challenge: staying up all night, or stopping wars.

As one of so many siblings, Catherine was a prime candidate for anorexia. She had good reason to fret over her own individuality, to hammer out a unique identity, to make herself autonomous. Living like a hermit was one way. Rigorous fasting—and it is said she lived seven years on her Communion regimen—was another. Like Elizabeth and many other saints who refused food, especially women, Catherine claimed fasting was a form of obedience, of submission. But it is quite the opposite. As eating is an act of will, starving on purpose is a stronger one.

Having damaged her health through years of fasting and other penances, the thirty-three-year-old Catherine suffered a

stroke in 1380. The stroke paralyzed her from the waist
down, and killed her eight days later. It is said that her last
words were, "Precious blood! Blood! Blood!"

ALLEGEDLY FRAGRANT AND flexible, the freshly dead
corpse was laid out in Santa Maria Sopra Minerva for several days. So many Romans flooded the church that an iron
screen was installed to protect Catherine's body from dismemberment. The sick were brought in great numbers, in
hopes that contact with the relics could cure them—or, fail-
ing direct contact, then with anything at all that had touched
the relics.

Before the body was to be entombed, one of Catherine's
longtime disciples kept vigil alongside it. First he cut locks of
hair from the corpse. Then he amputated a finger. He extracted a tooth. Others who had been close to Catherine jostled
for their own bits of her. Teeth started making the rounds.
Another disciple received the finger on which Catherine had
believed she wore Christ's betrothal ring.

After asking the dead woman for her "permission," Pope
Urban approved the removal of Catherine's head. It was cer-
emonially detached, inserted in a gilded copper reliquary and
taken to Siena in secret. After its arrival, a vast celebration
was staged to welcome the head.

In 1430, the headless corpse was installed in a new tomb
under Catherine's carved and painted likeness. The tomb was
opened frequently so that relics could be severed from the
body and parceled out to churches that desired them. A
church in England received containers packed with dust that
had once been skin. A rib went to Florence. A foot went to
Venice. A shoulder blade was given away. Second-class relics
were distributed as well: Catherine's shoe, and her flagellum,
and the metal chain with which she used to thrash herself.

❖

ON A SUNNY street north of Rome in Siena, the house where Catherine Benincasa grew up was turned after her death into a shrine. Visitors eagerly kissed the stairs. Today the house still lures pilgrims. Inside these walls, in this medieval hill town, Catherine's father had his dyeworks. In the house, now open to the public, is Catherine's tiny cell. Paintings and sculptures on display show scenes from her life; available for visitors' perusal are the saint's scant personal possessions. Nearby, in the Church of St. Dominic, peering mournfully from its vessel, is Catherine's head.

IT IS ONLY natural that her hometown would want to enshrine not an arm or a rib but her head.

Defying the barriers her time and place imposed, illiterate Catherine has been named not just a saint but also a Doctor of the Church. This is a title bestowed on only the most erudite writers, held by some two dozen male saints and only three women—Catherine, Teresa of Ávila, and Therese of Lisieux.

Her body, however, remained in Rome. Its allegedly incorrupt condition makes the spectacle of Catherine's decapitation grosser still. Another curious fact is that the Church of Santa Maria Sopra Minerva where she lies was, as its name reveals, erected over an ancient temple to a Roman goddess.

She was the goddess of not only war but of intellect.

CATHERINE'S ARE NOT the only bones in this church. In a tiny chapel against the wall where you'd hardly notice it is another glass-fronted casket. An electric candelabra illuminates the chapel but only faintly. Two of its six bulbs are lit. Behind the glass you can barely make out a skeleton. Dressed in a fluffy white frock with a golden belt, the skeleton looks like a child's. Someone has posed it carefully. Lying along one side, propped on one elbow, it rests its small skull in one hand as if in thought. Wreathed in pale blue silk roses, the skull is veiled. Its eye sockets and empty nostrils make long shadows on the filmy lace. Its cuffs are large, piratical against the girlish dress. A tiny light glimmers inside the casket. It illuminates the free hand poised over one hip clutching a frond.

The chapel's ceiling is painted to look like a sky, with golden stars and dots like little planets. The skeleton's feet wear small embroidered slippers.

How did this girl get here?

A dusty placard propped in front of the casket reads *Santa Wittoria—Martire*. Martyr. Although I have never heard of any saint by that name, this is possibly a strange spelling of the obscure St. Victoria who appears on a list of martyrs' relics sold in Rome by a famous dealer in the year 835.

A priest is chatting with friends in the church. The men's sharp voices ring against the stone, and I interrupt to ask him who this is.

He points over the railing to the sign. "A martyr," says the priest. He nods and glides away, like this is all we know and all we need to know.

A Haircut

▼▼▼▼

ST. PHILIP NERI
Chiesa Nuova (Santa Maria in Vallicella)
Rome, Italy

iN TERMINI STATION, ten-year-old boys drift back and
forth beside the public telephones. Their hands float at the
level of our pockets, we who use the phones. They wait for
one of us to look away. Their eyes meet mine as if to say *I'm
just doing my job.* They glide like sharks who can't stop
swimming or they'll drown.

Outside a magazine shop in the station stands a little prostitute. Just barely five feet tall, wearing a skintight Spandex
skirt, she stands quite still, holding the wall, soliciting. She's
blind. Under her copper hair her eyeballs are pure white. Her
delicate head swivels as she speaks.

A woman walking down the steps into the Metro wears a T-shirt that says *Screamin' Orgasm—How Many Can You Have and Still Walk?*

ST. PHILIP NERI used to roam these streets with half his beard shaved off. He'd put on funny clothes. He'd sidle up to boys and say, "So, friend, when shall we begin to do good?"

Rome had been sacked in 1527 and the Church was reeling from the lashings of the Reformation. Philip played the clown.

HE HAD DONE so as a child in Florence. He came from a distinguished line of Florentines but when his father offered him a copy of his own impressive family tree, Philip ripped it up. No one was sure what would become of him.

Having studied the humanities, he left home at sixteen to work for a business owned by his father's cousin. Philip did so well that his relative decided to make him his heir. Yet whenever he had a spare moment Philip withdrew to a little chapel in the mountains overlooking the sea.

At eighteen, Philip abruptly walked away from his job. Taking only the clothes on his back, he trekked all the way to Rome. By the time he arrived he was penniless. But presently he met a fellow Florentine who offered Philip room and board and a small salary in exchange for tutoring his two young sons. Philip taught the boys while studying philosophy and writing poetry—which later upset him so much that he burned it.

He took to visiting patients in Rome's hospitals, exhorting them to save their souls. He also loitered in shops, banks, warehouses, and other public venues preaching to strangers. Attracted to locales where young men could be found, he loved to linger in the streets telling jokes which he interspersed with sermons. Many found him irresistible. A pair of goldsmiths and the boys working in their shop were among the first to declare themselves Philip's disciples.

Focusing his evangelical efforts on men and boys, Philip was so tormented by what he described as the devil's temptations that he wondered whether he ought to flee into the mountains and dwell in total solitude. But a vision of John the Baptist persuaded him to stay in Rome, as did another vision in which two souls in heaven gave him the same message. One of them was eating a roll at the time. Keeping a vow of chastity, Philip wept, it is said, for the sins of his former years. He praised his cat for its virginity. A prostitute once tried to corner him but he fled down a stairwell as she hurled a footstool at his head.

Though he made friends easily, his personal regimen was as austere as a hermit's. In his sparse room he ate only one meal every day—and it was only water, bread, and olives. He beat himself with chains. His room held little besides a clothesline and a bed, and Philip eschewed the bed in order to sleep on the floor. Some nights he did not sleep at all but roamed the city, praying at his favorite haunts, including Rome's catacombs, the miles of subterranean tunnels where early Christians met in secret and buried their dead.

Late one night in 1544, Philip was alone in the catacombs of San Sebastiano—which are notable for having briefly housed the relics of saints Peter and Paul. Philip was deep in prayer when he saw what appeared to be a flaming ball hovering before his face. In an instant it leaped into his mouth. Searing his throat so that he thrashed and tore at his clothing, it descended to his chest. There it lodged, as Philip's shrieks rang through the underground chambers. Later he would recall having shouted, "Enough, Lord, enough! You're going to kill me with happiness!"

As the pain subsided he sat in the cool tunnel shaking viclently. Pressing his hand to his chest under his ripped shirt he was startled to discover a huge swelling the size of a peach.

It was to remain there all his life.

A layman and not a priest, Philip is said to have converted dozens of dissolute boys on a single day. After finally becoming ordained at the age of thirty-six in 1551, he promptly found his element: the confessional.

Sitting behind the screen he read penitents' minds like a true telepath. Many later reported that Philip had begun to describe their most secret sins before they had uttered a word. He is said to have once produced a clear vision of hell in a young nobleman's mind, at which point the young man changed his ways. At Philip's church of San Girolamo, from daybreak to noon, boys and men waited in long lines to confess. Some days, he had already heard dozens of confessions in his own room even before dawn.

Believing that the youths who sought him out needed even more guidance than he could give them in the confessional, Philip hosted afternoon and evening discussions and readings. He kept them busy with spiritual homework and physical chores such as stringing rosaries and moving furniture.

His attractiveness to other men is unquestionable, mentioned by biographer after biographer. Remembering Philip, the nobleman Fabrizio de' Massimi later wrote: "He won me over in so wonderful a way that I could afterward never leave him. He always went with me in my coach . . . and he led me to follow him, a thing I have never done for anyone else, by his caresses and demonstrations of affection."

Another friend, Tiberio Ricciardelli, once complained to Philip that he was troubled by persistent temptations. The priest seized him in a tight hug, pressing his breast to Ricciardelli's breast. The latter professed that his troubles had disappeared with this embrace. Others reported similar hugs.

A Haircut

▼▼▼▼▼

Philip's biographers spotlight the saint's remorse for past sins, his love of dressing up in outrageous outfits. It is hard not to wonder whether this is their way of hinting that the saint was gay.

Certainly in his dealings with women the saint was more reticent. Though he is hailed for having miraculously saved some from dying in childbirth, he also distrusted female churchgoers' emotional displays—pointing out that prostitutes were always the first to burst out weeping during mass. He felt women should be spoken to briefly and without a hint of sweetness. One day he met a man who was distraught because his little daughter had died.

"Idiot," Philip reportedly berated him. "Why are you upsetting yourself? Be quiet. You will soon have a boy."

PHILIP'S APPEARANCES IN church were associated with increasingly weird phenomena. Rays of light are said to have appeared out of nowhere, and rooms in which he was preaching were said to vibrate. Becoming suddenly ecstatic, Philip would leap around the pulpit. He dreaded these episodes, terrified that he would one day drop the communion wafers. One day during a fit on the pulpit he bit a chalice so hard that his teeth left marks on the rim. Then again, sometimes he had spells in which he lay rigid and motionless for hours, as if he was dead.

He often complained that his heart felt as if it was on fire—that it was emitting actual sparks. He had himself bled, thinking the procedure would cool the heat in his chest.

Philip was convinced that God gave him these fits and hot spells. But some researchers today suggest that the problem was purely physiological. Heart palpitations, which occurred over the years following Philip's strange experience in the catacomb, might well have sparked these altered states.

Nevertheless, Philip's colleagues envied his frequent departures into what they believed was a heavenly realm.

He told them their envy would vanish if they knew how his episodes felt.

HE WAS GETTING a reputation—for drama and hilarity as well as holiness. He would order penitents to take his large dog for a walk. Philip stipulated that the animal itself was not to do any walking. The penitents must carry it in their arms through the crowded city streets, making a public spectacle.

They said wherever he went felt like a party.

One day, as the story goes, he met a man who was condemned to die yet remained defiantly unrepentant. Rather than attempting to cajole the man, Philip seized him by the collar and hurled him bodily to the ground. It is said that the man repented at once.

Similarly Philip was known to grab people by their hair, their ears, their clothing, and even to hit them, while insisting that he was "hitting the devil, not you."

As a lark he wore his clothes inside out, donned enormous white shoes with his cassock and asked fellow clerics to read joke books aloud to him. Once he had his hair cut in church, during services. And during a solemn procession in 1590 featuring the relics of saints Papias and Maurus, Philip reached over in full view of the assembled crowd and pulled a Swiss guard's beard.

He admitted that some of his wackier stunts—the haircut in church, for example—were an attempt to distract himself from the spiritual intensity that always triggered his ecstasies.

TODAY PHILIP'S BODY lies behind glass in an elaborate chapel in the church of Santa Maria in Vallicella, also known as Chiesa Nuova, the "new church," not far from the Tiber.

A Haircut

▼▼▼▼▼

On the day I visit, six tiers of scaffolding form a grid over the entrance to his chapel in the left transept. Two men on the uppermost tier repair a sculpted angel's golden wing in silence. Philip had wanted the church to be plain, whitewashed, in keeping with the Counter-Reformation climate. But in the years following his death as Catholicism regained its ascendancy the church was steadily swathed in frescoes, mosaics, and marble. It is heavy with baroque touches and looks anything but ascetic. Frescoes leap across the ceiling, including one finished in 1644 by Pietro da Cortona which depicts a mystical vision Philip once had: the Virgin Mary swoops in and saves the faithful from a church on the verge of collapse. Three paintings by Rubens adorn the high altar—when I arrive they are sheathed in opaque plastic sheeting marked *Restauro*.

A wooden cross is mounted on the plastic and below it hangs a poster of the Virgin standing on a sickle moon.

The plastic over the paintings in the church rises and falls ever so slightly in the warm breeze rolling in from the street. From behind it comes the sound of a woman talking on a telephone. She is talking about the restoration, about paint and someone's schedule, someone named Camillo.

Si. Va bene. No. Sharp footsteps, pacing.

No, she cries. It echoes through the church.

IN PHILIP'S CHAPEL, a big mosaic shows him with his arms outstretched. Mother-of-pearl and coral disks as big as Ritz crackers form patterns up and down dark marble walls. A real wax candle, not a plugged-in one, burns in a sconce. Set deep inside a niche in one wall, the body lies behind a thick bronze grille. It wears a gold-encrusted robe of pure white satin. Hands gone dark with death rest on the robe, their knuckles prominent. The case is lined in red. A golden hoop over the crimson velvet pillow makes a halo. Philip's head is coated in thin silver; the effect is like one of the saint's own jokes. A man comes in and kneels. He prays. The woman on the phone is howling.

ON THE NIGHT after Philip died in 1595, doctors gathered to examine his corpse. They were eager to investigate the swelling on his chest. Some suspected it as a tumor. But upon opening his chest cavity, they saw something else entirely. His heart and pulmonary artery were swollen to twice their normal size. To accommodate the bulk, two ribs had burst away from the cartilage that normally connects them to the breastbone. They formed an arch. The examiners wrote medical treatises on the subject.

One year after Philip's death, an eternal flame burned at his tomb, which was surrounded by ex-votos from rich and poor alike. In 1599, Philip's surviving sister gave permission for the tomb to be opened. Its vestments had rotted away to fragments. But the body had been embalmed soon after death, which accounted for the remarkable preservation of its legs. Philip's face had not survived the years intact, so a silver mask in his likeness was crafted and fitted over the skull to take its place. Philip had predicted cryptically, years before, that someday his head would be "covered in silver."

Work began the following year on the chapel where he now lies on display. Two years later the room's gemstone inlay was complete, and jewelers estimated its value at more than seventy thousand English pounds. In 1922, the corpse was dressed in a new set of vestments and put on display.

The mother-of-pearl and coral lend the chapel a tropical ambience that feels un-Roman and even, for all its monetary value, whimsical—like an ecclesiastical Trader Vic's. Philip's last resting place is, in its own lavish way, decorated as he might like it: for a party.

Not a Fairy Tale

▼▼▼▼▼

ST. MARIA GORETTI
Our Lady of Graces
Nettuno, Italy

IN ROME I return to my lodgings one evening with a shopping bag full of cheap macaroons and exotic lettuce. The front door opens to a cloud of acrid smoke. No one is home. I fumble through the dark apartment past the snapshots of my hostess to the kitchen. Smoke swirls from a big pot on the stove. My hostess has forgotten to turn it off.

The pot is filled with fishheads. Now burned black, their pointed snouts breathe smoke. My hostess returns, bearing mushrooms in a jar. She smiles and licks her fever sore and fans the air.

❖

FROM ROME IT is an hour's train ride to Nettuno. Named for the sea god, Nettuno lies serene under a clear sea sky, its scalloped sands dotted with parasols and folding beach chairs. Bombed to smithereens in World War II, its neat right-angled streets are lined with sparkling concrete. On the esplanade, gelato shops stand side by side under awnings like open clamshells.

Right on the beach, Our Lady of Graces has been restored in postwar style. The sanctuary is a vast angular bulwark sprawling low against the shore. With its sleek simplicity, it brings to mind suburban synagogues I attended as a child in LA. The sea light falls, generous, along its length.

Inside the church, a staircase descends to the crypt. Its subterranean walls are all pale gray slabs of poured concrete. On one wall, a wooden Christ is beardless and bald and roughly hewn, evoking Polynesian war canoes. Two rows of varnished benches march across the floor.

Encased in sculpted wax to effect a fresh but spotless corpse, the remains of St. Maria Goretti wear a long white gown of cheap sateen. The dress shines softly over waxen hips and legs which are too small to match the figure's waxen head and large wax hands.

Murdered in 1902, Maria is the victim in Catholicism's biggest twentieth-century sex crime—a would-be rape that turned into a vicious stabbing.

She is also upheld as a model for the youth of today.

Emerging from puffy white sleeves, the hands gleam as if brushed with something viscous. Their splayed fingers are poised to hover awkwardly above Maria's thighs—a pose that draws a visitor's gaze directly and inescapably to her crotch. The fingers do not point but frame a flat and boneless-looking groin. It is a gesture somewhere between reverence and defense.

The waxen face gleams, with thick sheaves of girlish

brown hair falling to either side. With its pointed nose and sensuous lips, the face is meant to be a pretty girl's. But its sculptor ought to be ashamed. The slick waxen skin is monochromatic, lacking the subtle texture variations of real flesh that can be seen in older examples of this art, for instance the waxwork in Paris hiding the relics of St. Vincent de Paul. This face meant to be Maria's is no more convincing than a department-store mannequin's.

ON THE BENCHES, pilgrims wait their turns to approach the casket. A fat child wearing shorts stands and walks forward with his father, who stuffs a bill in the collection box before the casket and kneels. The boy makes a fist and knocks the glass. It resounds through the crypt. His father cuffs him.

"Look," the child shouts in Italian, "her finger broke off and they glued it back on."

It's true. The repair shows.

Maria's casket is glass on both sides so that you can see all the way through to the wall behind. It stands on a pedestal whose cement flanks were pocked repeatedly with some pointed tool when soft. Pilgrims have pressed snapshots and notes into the seams where the casket's metal frames meet the glass. Some have found a space through which they were able to stuff their snapshots all the way inside. Pictures lie scattered around the corpse, some upside-down, like gargantuan confetti. One of them shows a gray-haired woman wearing a turtleneck sweater with an appliquéd Christmas tree on the chest.

Two women set down their handbags before the casket and with white handkerchiefs they lovingly wipe the glass clean. Dark curls pulled back behind their ears, they kneel a long time.

*

MARIA GORETTI WAS a peasant girl who lived in a
swampy backwater near Nettuno. The Gorettis were so poor
that they shared a house with another family, the Serenellis.

A young man of twenty, Alessandro Serenelli had spent
years as a sailor before coming to help his elderly father run
the farm. It is said that he used to lie awake listening to his
elder brother and his sister-in-law having sex in another room.

On the farm, Alessandro began assembling a collection of
erotic books and magazines. He decorated his room with pictures of women. Soon he found himself unable to keep his
eyes off Maria. Nicknamed Marietta, the twelve-year-old
looked mature for her age. Preparing and serving the
Serenellis' meals were among her daily chores.

Maria was a pious child who chattered happily to
whomever would listen about Jesus and the saints. She can
only have been stunned when Alessandro, catching her alone
one day, said he wanted her.

She replied that she had no idea what he meant.

Alessandro slunk off, brooding. But there would be a
next time.

One day in July, Maria made lunch for the household.
After eating, the parents of both families slipped away for
their afternoon naps. Maria sat on the landing at the top of
the staircase that led to the house. Her baby sister Teresa rested on a plank in the kitchen.

At three o'clock, Alessandro appeared. From the bottom
of the stairs he asked if she might mend his torn shirt. When
she agreed, he mounted the steps. Slipping past her on the
landing he darted into the kitchen. She followed, only to see
that he had seized a weapon: not an ordinary knife as in
most depictions of the crime, it was a special hook used in
making brushes.

He jumped her.

Wielding his blade, Alessandro was all over Maria. She cried out to God, shouting that she would rather die than give Alessandro what he wanted. The rebuffed youth stabbed her fourteen times. When both families rushed in, they found Maria huddled in a messy pool of her own blood mixed with viscera. Her stomach and chest torn open, she was still alive.

She begged them to keep Alessandro away. But he was nowhere to be seen. He had fled.

On a litter, Maria was carried to Nettuno's hospital. News of the crime raced across the countryside. Alessandro, discovered hiding in his room, was arrested. By the time doctors completed emergency surgery on Maria's perforated heart, lungs, and intestines, a crowd had gathered outside. Sheaves of flowers arrived for her.

After the surgery, she gave police a full report of the crime from her hospital bed, but insisted that she had forgiven her assailant. She wanted Alessandro's soul, she said, to join hers in heaven.

It wasn't long before peritonitis set in.

With her mother at her bedside, Maria died in the hospital. From all over the region, thousands of people poured into town to attend a funeral for a girl whom they had never met, never seen, of whom they had never heard until the preceding day. Nettuno's shops shut down for the event, as they might for a holiday. The crowds, who did not know this girl, went wild with grief.

ALESSANDRO EXPRESSED NO remorse during the trial in which he was swiftly convicted and sentenced to thirty years. He was to spend the first three in solitary confinement, the rest at hard labor.

One night in jail, he had a dream. A beautiful girl in a white dress was strolling toward him across a garden, picking white lilies. As she drew closer he saw that it was Maria. Radiant, she gave him fourteen flowers: one for each of her stab wounds. When he awoke, a terrible guilt barraged him for the first time since the killing.

Alessandro became a model prisoner. Professing himself devout ever since the night of his strange dream, he began exchanging letters with a bishop. In one, he described his crime as "a strangely fated moment of mental aberration" during which he was "impelled by passion beyond my control."

Maria's murder had grabbed headlines, as had Alessandro's trial. Long afterward, the story continued to make news. In 1910, eight years after the murder, Pope Pius X publicly declared Maria the "twentieth century's St. Agnes." He was alluding to the fourth-century martyr who vowed to preserve her virginity but then died after being stabbed in the throat.

Alessandro left prison after twenty-seven years. Three years had been cut from his sentence for good behavior. Retreating from the outside world he entered a Capuchin monastery as a lay brother, tending its garden. Maria's mother, Assunta Goretti, had long since forgiven him. One Christmas, she attended church alongside her daughter's killer.

One day in the spring of 1947, a woman in Rome lay gravely ill with pleurisy. Familiar with Maria's story, she began praying to the dead girl for a cure and was rewarded, it is claimed, with good health. A few days later a workman, also in Rome, injured his foot severely. Later he would insist that his prayers to Maria had brought about a full recovery.

Her beatification process began.

Witnesses came forth and testified to Maria's saintliness. Alessandro was one of them, recounting the murder in detail. Maria's bones were exhumed from their grave in a cemetery near her home. A waxwork was fashioned to contain them.

In this form, her relics traveled from church to church throughout northern Italy. Crowds lined up for a chance to see them.

Maria's canonization ceremony in June 1950 attracted a record-breaking throng to Rome. Maria's mother and her siblings were in the crowd.

WATCHING ME INSPECT Maria's sarcophagus in the crypt at Nettuno, a church custodian follows me up the stairs.

"Did you pray?" he demands. He takes my silence as a yes.

"A foreigner?" he asks. He strides along the corridor toward the gift shop like a party host. The corridor is lined with books in many different languages about the murder, with lurid dime-novel covers. On one, a hulking shadow looms across a kitchen floor. On another, a fist grips a knife. On a less literal cover, a flower spurts blood as a knife plunges between its petals.

The titles are spattered with Zip-a-tone blood.

The Crimson Lily.

Murder in the Swamp.

IN A LARGE room at the end of the corridor, before we reach the gift shop, glass cases display artifacts of Maria's life and death. Among these are hanks of Maria's hair, her death certificate, a dress she wore. Her autopsy cloth is a grisly memento, and a metal canister is labeled as that which held her bones between 1938 and 1947. A photograph shows Pope John Paul II with the waxwork. On his visit in 1979, he paid a visit to Teresa Goretti, who as a baby witnessed her sister's murder and later became a Franciscan nun.

Posted along one wall are the pages of a comic book telling Maria's story.

"Can you read Italian?" asks the custodian, speaking

Italian, swaying comfortably in his baggy pants. He jabs a finger at a word balloon.

"Not really."

"Well, then, I'll read it to you," he announces in Italian, as if the problem is that I am illiterate. He rushes to the first page. Patting the wall and reading the text aloud he adds his own running commentary.

"Here she is praying to the Virgin," he offers, shouting at the top of his lungs as one does when speaking to the ignorant.

Maria kneels, her eyes uplifted.

"Here's her father's funeral."

A casket is being carried to a cemetery. "Life was very hard for them after that, you understand, very hard."

Maria sweeps a kitchen, dressed in rags like Cinderella.

"See how poor they were? 'Doing domestic tasks,'" the man reads carefully.

"She visited this very church on market days. She took communion and she knew the catechism all by heart." He rubs his head.

Maria sits on the staircase repairing a shirt. Alessandro appears. She rebuffs him, he assaults her. You can sort of see the top half of his butt. His knee is raised. A knife is on the counter, the way they often are.

"She defended herself energetically. 'I'd rather die than consent,'" the custodian shouts.

A lynch mob hunts for Alessandro. Cute as ever, Maria lies dying in Nettuno's hospital.

Wearing the striped pajamas of a prison inmate, Alessandro dreams. His chin is drawn enormous, bigger than his brow, a head shaped like a fleshy boomerang.

"A miracle," cries the custodian. In Alessandro's dream, the dead Maria brings him flowers. She looks pointedly unsexual.

The murderer repents; his victim's mother pardons him

then dies in 1954, says the custodian. He lifts his leg and scratches it.

IN THE CRYPT, Maria's waxen breasts under her high-necked dress are tiny buds. She wears a glittering but cheap tiara.

She lies like Sleeping Beauty charmed—like Snow White whom the dwarfs encased in glass. And yet it is no prince's kiss for which Maria waits. No royal wedding for this girl, no castle. Her story is not a fairy tale although the faithful insist that its ending is happy. Maria's corpse, crowned, is not that of a princess who might waken but an ordinary girl. She chose death over rape; her "holy purity" has left her dead at twelve years old.

Most girls at twelve live in a kind of daze, not certain what they look like or who might be looking or the dreams that come with looking, though they do suspect. What was Maria thinking when she first turned Alessandro down? She must have loathed those charged days afterward. As she watched him watch her, she probably longed to disappear.

THIS GIRL WAS canonized because she chose death. On one hand she was defiant. On the other hand, she's dead. What then does Maria's canonization mean for rape victims who live to tell the tale? That they are less to be pitied for choosing to live? That they in fact are to be blamed, even called cowards or sluts, because unlike the saint they let themselves be fouled?

In anthology after anthology of saints' stories for children, Maria is hailed as a "model for the youth of today." Drawings depict her as rosily beautiful, haloed, her palms pressed together in prayer. Her dark eyes gaze upward with all the helpless and unintelligent innocence of a fawn's. She has been named the patron saint of all teenage girls. When Pope John Paul II visited Nettuno in 1979, he gave a speech urging young Catholics to remember Maria's purity and to let it help steer them through the modern world.

All young girls are exhorted to take Maria as their role model. Yet only a small minority, hopefully, will ever be assaulted by would-be rapists. Maria's story cannot possibly apply to *all* girls—unless you extract from her story the message that all premarital sex is in varying degrees a form of rape. While Alessandro might be crueler than your average man, still he exemplifies the fact that men just press, press, press and virgins must resist. The sainting of Maria blurs the border between rape and willing acts. Her fame commemorates the awful things men do to little girls but it does not stop there.

POTTED PLANTS FLANK the casket. Votive lamps give off a faint electric glow. The cement echoes every murmured prayer.

A sign says that the waxwork contains "the prime parts" of Maria's body. These include her skull, spinal column, and more, though an arm bone was removed from the corpse and given to Maria's grieving mother. Finger bones and other small bits were distributed in the years following Maria's death as relics to other churches.

They say outliving your own child is the most excruciating ordeal life has to offer. Watching your dead child turned into a saint adds an unimaginable dimension. Surviving her daughter by more than forty years, Assunta Goretti was compelled to visit Maria's remains not in a graveyard but a shrine.

A teenage girl wearing bell bottoms held fast with a belt made of linked steel hoops kneels to touch the glass. Her nails are painted navy blue. Her hair is bleached an icy white. She trails her fingers back and forth over Maria's face, a clutch of plastic bangles clacking softly at her wrist. Then she crosses herself with the same hand. Her stretch top hikes up in back, showing a white mandorla of her skin.

On one bench, someone has carved *Antonio* into the varnish with a knife and, under this, a phone number.

Helen Goes Shopping

▼▼▼▼

ST. THOMAS
Santa Croce in Gerusalemme
Rome, Italy

Swathed in white tarps and crisscrossed with scaffolds, the church of Santa Croce in Gerusalemme overlooks a swirl of traffic whose stop-and-start rhythm is hypnotic.

In the busy road fronting the church, an aging man with a fine suntan is begging alms. He wears a yellow golf shirt crisply pressed, with eelskin loafers and smart doubleknits. A wooden cross hangs on a cord around his neck. His hair combed over, sweat and sunlight glitter on his scalp. The day is hot, so all the drivers idling at the red light have their windows down. He scuttles to the nearest car, thrusting his head and shoulders through the window, reaching in to stroke the driver's hand. Ignored, he hurries to a Porsche in which a businessman sits staring straight ahead. A woman in a Lamborghini looks away but gives the man a bill. Most of the drivers jerk their arms away and try to shut their windows as the man's cross clacks the steel. A white van pulls to a stop and the beggar's hands flutter toward the driver, a young man with earrings. A phoenix is tattooed on the young man's arm and he turns and glares and starts to scream just as the traffic starts to move.

SANTA CROCE IN Gerusalemme got its rococo façade in 1744. But the church was begun much earlier—around the year 320, under the auspices of Constantine the Great. He was doing his mother a favor.

The saint formerly known as Empress Helen was a devout Christian. She had married Emperor Diocletian's left-hand man, who defended the empire's western borders against invading tribes. The couple's son Constantine was born in 274.

While Christianity found a smattering of adherents in Rome shortly after Jesus's death, it remained a minor fringe cult. The empire was pervasively pagan, though its paganism was gloriously diverse. Christianity did not hold a candle to other mystical Middle Eastern imports such as Mithraism, whose all-male followers worshiped a god of light. Isis was immensely popular. And ecstatic youths castrated themselves in devotion to the Phrygian goddess Cybele.

But with its promise of heaven, Christianity appealed to those Romans who weren't getting much out of life on earth: slaves and women.

Perhaps because Christians seemed to lack any sense of humor, Diocletian singled them out for public ridicule, which regularly included torture. Indulging the Christians' craving for martyrdom, Diocletian had them beheaded, buried alive, shot full of arrows, or thrown to the lions. In this manner, during this period, Christianity gained many of its most famous saints. But worship was carried on underground, in the catacombs. Rome's persecuted Christians met in secret.

When Helen's husband Constantius Chlorus died at York in 306, his army swiftly declared his son Constantine the new emperor. Six years later, Constantine's forces were battling rivals on the Tiber just outside Rome. Greatly outnumbered, Constantine's men are said to have witnessed a flaming cross hovering in the sky—and promptly won a startling victory. Constantine was following in his mother's spiritual footsteps. One year after the battle, his Edict of Milan officially sanctioned Christianity throughout the empire. Christians crept out of the closet with a vengeance. Constantine went on to establish Constantinople, his own new capital east of the old one. As basilicas popped up here and there, altering the skyline, Constantine made Christianity the official state religion.

Helen made a pilgrimage to the Holy Land in search of relics to buy and bring home. An old woman by this time, she spent a lot of money. Critics through the centuries have mocked Helen as an easy target for the squadrons of counterfeit relic-sellers who, often disguised as monks, peddled animal bones and other fakes to willing pilgrims. Nevertheless her prodigious purchases later spread all over Europe. Among the largest was a towering marble staircase said to come from Pontius Pilate's house in Jerusalem. Now it stands in the middle of Rome across from San Giovanni in Laterano near the Esquiline Hill. Busloads of pilgrims arrive to climb the stairway on their knees.

SOME OF HELEN'S most highly prized purchases reside across the city at Santa Croce in Gerusalemme. Inside the church, behind its rococo façade, are marble columns the pinkish gray of fish roe. Hanging among these is a painting in which the resurrected Jesus greets onlookers who spread their arms in wonder. Only one man in the crowd holds back. Thomas the Apostle looks skeptical, unsure that what he sees is real. Swathed in a scarlet robe that reaches to his Roman sandals, he lifts his finger to touch the wound in Christ's side. In its Book of John, the New Testament has him saying, "Unless I see . . . and touch . . . I will not believe." Gory as it was, that touch told "doubting Thomas" what he wanted to know.

To the left of the church's high altar is its Chapel of Relics. In its entryway a chunk of wood is labeled *Pars Crucis Boni Latronis*, allegedly part of the cross to which the "good thief" was nailed near the crucified Jesus. Severe angles and slick gray marble in the chapel hint at fascist tastes, with sharp architectural details bespeaking *Raiders of the Lost Ark*. Inlaid marble in the walls is made to look like candlesticks burning before trompe-l'oeil curtains. A siren screams past, outside the lofty window.

The chapel is as hot as a sauna. A tall glass pavilion resting on black marble columns in the middle of the room holds the relics. Three Italian pilgrims, a woman and two men, are taking turns posing in front of it for photographs. They trade a camera back and forth. Standing before the glass that shields Thomas's fingerbone and a thorn from the Crown of Thorns, nails from the Passion and splinters of the True Cross, they grimace, unsure what expression is appropriate. They are happy to be here. The woman bounces in her flowered gauze dress. Yet they know it might not be right to smile next to nails that pierced Christ.

In the glass case, reliquaries compete for space. One is gold and shaped like a cross. A bas-relief adorns it in which Jesus calmly rips open his chest cavity to reveal a heart pierced all over with swords—like toothpicks at a cocktail party, like the Three of Swords penetrating a heart in the Tarot deck. The reliquary's crystal windows reveal three wooden chips. Standing nearby, another reliquary houses a mean-looking thorn.

Yet another is shaped like a tongue depressor, with metal leaves enclosing a tiny metal cage. Inside the cage are the bones of a human finger. In a city of relics this is one of the most adored: allegedly the finger of Thomas himself. Having actually touched Jesus, give or take a few layers of epidermis, these bones are among the most highly prized in all of Christendom.

In a corner of the chapel is a tiny door no bigger than a Ouija board. Its size is baffling. Inches off the floor its heavy padlock hangs, as if the chapel has a separate entryway only for elves.

LEAVING THE CHAPEL I return to the main part of the church. A painting of St. Lucy shows the young girl displaying her torn-out eyes on a plate. She tore them out, her legend says, to dissuade an amorous pagan who had praised them. Whether or not that is true, records show that Lucy was probably stabbed in the throat during the reign of Diocletian. In the painting, although two blue eyes lie gleaming on the plate, Lucy gazes heavenward nevertheless, not with empty bleeding sockets but with *eyes*, as if she has sprouted a new pair the way an injured starfish grows new legs.

During my half hour in the chapel, the church has become crowded. Its large door keeps opening to the roar of traffic outside as men and women enter. Dressed as for a party, they seem to know one another, embracing lightly and murmuring and filling the pews.

Near the ceiling, a sculpted angel weeps, clutching the Crown of Thorns as if he has flown home having taken it as a souvenir. With his free hand, the angel shields his eyes.

The new arrivals in the church are wearing elegant dresses and suits and summer hats, mostly in black. Another painting in their midst shows St. Rita of Cascia clasping her hands to her chest. Hers are not dainty fingers but resemble pale garlic sausages. Christ hovers over her. Cartoonish as if painted by a child, he makes a red mark on her head: stigmata. A group of men comes in carrying a coffin. Its polished wooden lid is piled high with moist chrysanthemums yellow as fire.

Cracking Whips

▼▼▼▼▼

St. Gaspare del Bufalo
Santa Maria in Trivio
Rome, Italy

Tourist-information kiosks are scattered all around Rome. I make a circuit of them, asking about relics. Mostly the staffers just say San Giovanni in Laterano has Peter's and Paul's heads—which it does, in shining gold reliquaries mounted practically too high to see. But after that they shrug. At the very idea a girl in a kiosk on the Tiber laughs, showing her midriff. In order to enter the pilgrims' information kiosk at St. Peter's Basilica I stand waiting for an hour behind barricades while the pope performs a blessing over newlyweds and the disabled. Then the officer in the kiosk says he cannot think of any relics offhand. But he says he knows of some nuns who just might sell me one.

Yet in one booth in the middle of nowhere a man wearing designer shades and a tailored silk shirt is very interested. He calls his old school friend who has become a priest.

"He'll know," the man says holding up one hand, his gold watch glinting in the light from passing cars.

"*Dove sono i corpi?*" shrieks the man. He scribbles notes across a sheet of stationery. "*Sì.*" His other phones ring but he doesn't answer them; his pen flits back and forth. The priest's voice buzzes through the phone.

A waifish boy in faded fatigues walks in asking for directions to the "Spanish Stairs." The man does not look up, points northward with his free hand till the boy goes.

THE MAN HAS sent me in search of a church near the Trevi Fountain where the bones of St. Gaspare rest. I cannot find this church. The fountain sings. Its blue water jets over tritons and white stone horses as a tour group from Japan slumps on the steps above it. Licking ice cream cones they stare at one another, blinking, as if they have stayed up all night, not having fun but ill. In a travel agency behind the fountain, where a sign in the window advertises sightseeing tours of Rome, the clerks are enjoying midmorning espressos while shouting at the top of their lungs about who should wash the tray. They sip their drinks from tiny steaming cups and say there is no such church as Santa Maria in Trivio.

"You want the Pantheon," they chime.

I don't.

They read the church's name just as the kiosk man has written it. They shake their chic heads confidently, swinging their hair. "No no no no."

Resigned to admiring Trevi Fountain, I find the church after having given up. Smothered in batting that appears as if it has hung here for years, Santa Maria's small portal seems more appropriate to some less hallowed venue, like a laundry.

The church is no less obscure than its permanent occupant. Banished once, later imprisoned, Roman-born Gaspare is hardly known in his own hometown.

SOON AFTER GASPARE'S birth in 1786, the fragile baby suffered from an eye disease. Calling it incurable, doctors told his parents to prepare themselves for life with a blind son. Hoping for a miracle, Gaspare's mother and father prayed to St. Francis Xavier. When the malady disappeared without a trace, their piety redoubled. They passed this on to Gaspare. The child became intensely religious, terrified of committing even the most casual and accidental of sins. He loathed his own strong will and the inclinations he decried as evil.

At fourteen he received his first tonsure, the ritual head-shaving that paved the way toward priesthood.

Ordained eight years later, he threw himself into missionizing among Rome's slums. From piazza to marketplace, he went after the souls of criminals and street people. The natural aggressiveness he so disliked helped to hone his preaching style which one witness called "a spiritual earthquake."

But politics got in his way. After the French Revolution, Napoleon Bonaparte claimed supreme leadership over most of Europe. Napoleon cherished the revolution's anti-clerical views, and regularly summoned priests to swear allegiance to him—an oath that Pope Pius VII strictly forbade. In 1810, Gaspare was called before a military assembly and ordered to swear allegiance. He refused. Threatened and cajoled, he gave the reply that constitutes what scant recognition he carries today: "*Non posso, non debo, non voglio*": I cannot, I should not, I will not.

For this he was banished from Rome along with other recalcitrant clergy. Imprisoned outside the city, he spent a four-year exile languishing in several dungeons. After Napoleon fell, Gaspare returned to a Rome that had been virtually without priests for five years. Desperate to make up for lost time, he gathered recruits and founded an evangelical brotherhood called the Archconfraternity of the Most Precious Blood.

The brothers roamed central Italy. From Tuscany to Umbria to Campania they lingered in the most squalid neighborhoods. While sin in general worried Gaspare, he felt that criminals' souls and those of the poor were at higher risk than ordinary people's.

His men staged public events as frequently as five times a day. These dramatic preaching extravaganzas lured beggars off the streets and thieves from their lairs to watch the brothers flagellate themselves. The sound of whips striking flesh echoed across piazzas until the assembled spectators trembled with excitement. Afterward, priests by the dozen gathered to hear confession.

THE ACT OF flagellation, used in civil law to punish slaves, grew popular in medieval times as a form of penance. In the fourteenth century organized groups of French, Flemish, and German flagellants would walk from town to town, whipping themselves while begging God to forgive the sins of the world. Ingmar Bergman used such a scene in *The Seventh Seal*. Viewing themselves as redeemers, the flagellants were laypersons but lived by strict rules—although some were later suspected of holding orgies in which scourging took part. When they arrived in a town, they assembled in the square and whipped themselves until they bled. Townspeople welcomed them, rushing forward to soak bits of cloth in the flagellants' blood. They kept these and used them as relics.

Convents and abbeys would reserve the practice for a special day each week, often Friday. One French nun wrote centuries ago of giving herself three hundred strokes for every genuflection. An Italian cardinal wrote an entire book in 1057 praising the discipline. Its popularity lasted until the 1960s.

GASPARE'S THEATRICS DREW gangs who streamed down from their mountain hideouts. Sometimes the criminals laid their firearms at Gaspare's feet, declaring that their lives of crime were over. Other spectators brought obscene books and other questionable items to be burned in a huge pyre. To signal their departure the priests would hoist a cross in the piazza while singing.

Devotees dubbed Gaspare *Il Santo*, the saint, and *Il Martello*, the hammer. But his success in converting gangs enraged politicians long accustomed to taking the criminals' bribes. Gaspare's new enemies-in-high-places pressured Pope Leo XII to suspend the priest. Leo demurred, calling Gaspare "an angel." The furious politicians then moved to have Gaspare sent far away to Brazil. This too failed.

IN 1836, WHEN Gaspare was weak with what would prove a fatal illness, he preached at the height of a cholera epidemic.

The disease swept Europe in waves, traveling by land and sea from Bengal. Each new outbreak killed thousands as the streets ran with infectious vomit and diarrhea. Retreating from the chaos of Rome's latest epidemic, Gaspare took to his bed. Preparing for death, he asked to be alone. Alternating between the chills and a terrible thirst, he shunned all offers of water.

❖

TODAY HIS REMAINS are hidden under a life-size bronze
sculpture that shows him lying dressed in priestly vestments,
as if freshly dead. One hand hangs limply at his side, fingers
splayed, as during Yul Brynner's death scene in *The King and
I*. Welded to Gaspare's head is a large flat halo like a soup
tureen. His actual relics cannot be seen.

The church dates back to the 6th century, when it was
built here by a penitent who'd fought the Ostrogoths. Rebuilt
completely in the 16th century by a student of Michelangelo,
it was officially given to Gaspare for the brotherhood. Its
smallness makes it dark, a gilded slit.

The only other person in the church is a young man wearing a T-shirt that says *Hoop King* with a photograph of
Michael Jordan. He is praying on his knees, the vinyl squeal-
ing as he moves. A painting shows Gaspare with a crucifix
tucked in his cummerbund, pressing his fingers to his breast.
Riding a cloud, he looks as if he is surfing. At his feet a red-
cloaked angel-boy holding a book stares at him, startled. But
a pink-gowned angel-girl, not to be caught off-guard, stands
calmly by and offers Gaspare a golden chalice overflowing
with what looks like blood.

Pope Pius XII was here in 1954 to canonize him. Holy
cards piled on a table near the door show the old pope standing beside the painting, framed by homely plants in vases on
the mantel.

Pilgrims claim that miracles occurred after they prayed
here—not only over Gaspare's relics but also those of his
associate, Don Giovanni Merlini. Not a saint yet, Merlini lies
near the wall, his bones and ashes currently obscured behind
the workmen's scaffolds.

On the altar are electric candles, thin and white, unlit.

Singsong Verses

▼▼▼▼▼

ST. FRANCIS XAVIER
Il Gesù
Rome, Italy

aT A CONSTRUCTION site on my way to the church called *Il Gesù*, a man wearing a dress suit and waiting for a bus is writing something with the tip of his umbrella in the wet sand left by a sudden rain.

Mario, he writes and stands back, proudly.

In a pizzeria across from the church, the chef leans on his counter chanting the names of his dishes. *Canneloni, funghi.* His injured right hand is bleeding heavily into the white gauze bandages wrapped loosely around it. With its bindings the hand is as big as a shoe.

He waves the hand, naming his prices.
It will be a day of hands, afflicted arms.

THE CHURCH'S PALE façade is stern. It does not prepare
you for the darkness inside—an expansive darkness, like
that of a village by night, whose farthest edge you cannot
see. All down this darkness, tiny bulbs and candles wink: the
fireflies in the sleeping village. Completed in 1584, this
Jesuit headquarters offered a radically new design, with an
aisleless nave so that the congregation could easily see the
priest on his pulpit.

A great baroque bulwark of gold and silver glints in the
glow of tiny perpetual lamps against one wall. It is St.
Ignatius Loyola's tomb, the largest I have ever seen. Atop it a
silver statue of Ignatius gazes skyward, flanked by marble
and gemstones and roiling swaths of precious metals like a
high night tide.

The church is the Jesuits' world headquarters, and he is
their founder—having persuaded his friends at the Sorbonne,
unordained and in the fullness of their youth, to take a
solemn vow of chastity.

As a young Basque soldier defending Pamplona against a
French siege, he sustained a cannonball blow. It shattered his
leg, and the gangly nobleman was constrained to endure a
long recuperation. Filling the long empty hours with books,
he decided to trade armor for clerical robes. He had no train-
ing in religion, so Ignatius began studying Latin as a
thirty-year-old among Barcelona schoolboys in 1524.

Traveling to Paris, he befriended seven young scholars in
the Latin Quarter. They listened intently to his dreams of
converting Moslems in faraway lands. Together, the friends
gathered one day in Montmartre and swore to remain chaste.

After they were ordained, Ignatius named his new group the Society of Jesus: the Jesuits. It wasn't long before the strangely intense priests drew attention—and accusations of heresy.

ACROSS THE DARKNESS from Ignatius's tomb is a green marble barrier protecting a delicate shrine. White electric tapers soar from gleaming candlesticks. The bulbs give out a wan and spectral glow that bathes a reliquary the size and shape of an hors d'oeuvres platter. Silver foliage in the reliquary daintily surrounds a human arm.

The arm is mounted upright like a bowling pin. A metal frame holds it in place. Thick sinews show through wizened skin the thin translucent brown of cockroach wings. Its wrinkled fist points ceilingward as if in a salute. *Right on.*

BORN IN A Spanish castle, Francis Xavier was deeply immersed in Paris's charms by the time he met Ignatius Loyola—a fellow Basque—at the University of Paris. Staying up late with the former soldier and his other new friends, Francis spent long hours discussing heaven and earth.

Hearing about the company he was keeping, Francis's parents in Spain were horrified. They arranged a comfortable job for their treasured youngest son back home in Pamplona. But too late: by the time their news reached his Parisian lodgings, Francis had already made his vow and cast his lot with Ignatius. They had left France and had gone to see the pope. Ordained, the brotherhood launched into its regimen of missionizing and practicing the "spiritual exercises" that Ignatius had developed as a way to experience the joy and pain of his favorite saints. Francis embraced it all so avidly that he collapsed from exhaustion in Bologna.

Portugal's King John III was searching for missionaries he

could send to India. The navigator Vasco da Gama had annexed India for John, and Portuguese traders were living there. But to a Catholic king, the state of India's souls sounded an alarm bell. Not only Hinduism but also Buddhism had sprung from Indian soil. That Indians were in his time, as now, among the world's most spiritual people only placed them in graver danger, he thought. Their spiritual pathways, to John's way of thinking, led them straight to hell.

The king asked a former University of Paris administrator if he could think of anyone who might be up to the task of converting all of India. Years before, this administrator had been so infuriated with Ignatius that he planned to have the former soldier flogged. Now he suggested that King John send Jesuits.

Asked to choose a missionary who could withstand a long stint among ignorant foreigners in a fetid climate, Ignatius selected a sturdy priest. When at the last minute the man fell sick and couldn't go, Ignatius turned to Francis. Scholarly and genteel, Francis could hardly enjoy the prospect, but Ignatius gave his old friend an order. Francis sailed away on his thirty-fifth birthday.

He learned very quickly that he was susceptible to seasickness.

The ship spent five months in Mozambique, sheltering from bad weather, before it reached India after a year's time.

Francis arrived at Goa on the southwestern coast in 1542, knowing nothing about the Indians except that they were Satan's slaves.

He used the social skills he'd honed in Paris years before. Mingling among Indians on the street, he ingratiated himself with the lower castes—knowing that his promises of a glorious afterlife would tempt them most of all. He played cards loitered on doorsteps, and strolled the beach with sailors.

fishermen, gamblers, and prostitutes. Presenting himself as a sincere new friend and confidant, he knew how to relax them, charm them, soften them, cajole. To Francis they "confessed" their "sins," though they may not have seen it that way.

Most of all, he targeted children. With his courtly bearing, Francis walked the lanes of Goa ringing a little bell. At its pretty sound, youngsters dropped their games and chores and darted from their homes. Like the Pied Piper leading the children of Hamelin, Francis led them to his church.

There he taught them singsong versions of the Hail Mary. Transformed into catchy jingles, prayers proved irresistible. In ever larger numbers, children came to learn and then parrot the songs, though they were not sure what the lyrics meant. Curious, their parents came as well.

Focusing on the bare-bones basics, Francis taught by means of rote repetition. He was also careful to include a vivid account of both heaven and hell. Hurriedly he baptized as many as possible—the total number is said to have reached into the tens of thousands.

Of these multitudes, only one convert is said to have been of the topmost caste, a Brahman. Francis found what he sought among the poor, the disenfranchised. Another bit of social history was in his favor. Into the flock came women whom Portuguese traders had raped. Disgraced, they had nowhere else to turn.

Not only the Brahman priests were proving an obstacle. Other communities thrived in Goa as well. In a letter to Portugal's King John, Francis wrote that "many live according to Jewish and Mohammedan law without any fear or shame." In another letter, he asked for permission to punish idolmakers with death.

"The natives of India," he wrote, "are so terribly wicked."

❖

TRAVELING UP AND down India's Malabar and
Coromandel coasts, Francis carried a parasol to guard
against the blazing sun. He spent three years among pearl
fishermen. Then he sailed on to Ceylon, to Malacca in western Malaysia, then to the "Spice Islands"—the Moluccas,
near New Guinea.

Seasickness wracked him every time.

Francis has been credited with a marvelous facility for
speaking in tongues. His legend also has him healing the sick,
raising the dead, and appearing in two places, far apart, at
one time. Yet scholars insist that in fact Francis was inept at
languages. In each new region he struggled to teach theolog-
ical concepts for which the local languages had no words. His
bungled translations baffled his listeners, sparking laughter.

Letters from Jesuits in Europe were the missionary's only
link to Europe and his past. And these were rare. In a missive
to Ignatius, Francis wistfully points out that but a single letter from the latter, his mentor, has arrived over the past four
years. Francis would never speak Spanish among Spaniards
again, much less Basque among Basques. He took to signing
his letters as "the least and loneliest of all your brothers."

Hoarding what scant correspondence he received, Francis
snipped his friends' signatures out of their letters. On a cord
he hung these scraps bearing their names next to his heart as
a pendant.

His sojourns put him in danger. En route to one island, a
fellow traveler warned Francis that the locals tended to poison strangers. Hearing this, he refused to carry an antidote.
Elsewhere Francis dodged gunfire, had his bed torched, and
fled hungry tigers.

Amid such primitive conditions, he longed for civilized
company. So when he met Yanjiro—a Japanese Christian

who described his homeland's high culture, code of honor, and brilliant scholars—Francis was excited. Said to have been the first Japanese ever baptized, Yanjiro agreed to act as Francis's guide.

A letter Francis wrote in 1548 describes his destination as "big islands, not long ago discovered." The Japanese, he believed, were "longing for knowledge."

A year later, Buddhist priests banned him from preaching to the locals in his broken Japanese.

In order to get what he wanted, Francis would have to make influential friends. In Kagoshima, on the island of Kyushu, Francis paid a hopeful visit to Lord Shimazu Takahisa's castle. He also met with Shinto and Buddhist officials. But Japan was clearly not a country where he could perform the wholesale conversions he had managed elsewhere. The Japanese debated him. They tore away at biblical loopholes. All his talk of demons did not move them. Visiting a *daimyo*, Francis rebuked the nobleman's well-known penchant for sodomy. As Francis's mortified translator delivered the rebuke, the daimyo listened calmly and then told them he had no intention of giving up what he loved.

Even Francis's clothes made him an outcast. Far from home, his cassock was faded and worn. While among low-caste Indians it had given him a look of solidarity, and advertised his priestly vow of poverty, tatters drew only scorn in Japan. Children openly mocked him—unlike their Indian counterparts. When he went to visit the emperor, Francis was turned away. Not only were his clothes unacceptable, but he had also failed to bring expensive gifts.

Francis pondered his problem. Foreign dress was trendy among Japan's elite. Many had taken to wearing European hats. Francis saw his solution: he must put away his cassock and disguise himself, for God.

Borrowing elegant garments from European friends, he dressed up as a Portuguese ambassador. Presenting himself as such, Francis arrived at a nobleman's palace. Well-prepared this time, he brought gifts which he had acquired from an Indian viceroy. These gifts were selected with an eye to what Francis knew the Japanese liked: mirrors, crystal, fabric, European clothing, spectacles, musical instruments, even a chiming clock. Bearing his imported treasures, the masquerading priest made his rounds among Japan's feudal lords.

During one of these visits, Francis staged an even more complicated charade. He had arranged for some Portuguese friends to arrive at the palace at a certain moment dressed in their finest clothes. When they arrived, their gold chains and pearl-studded hats glimmering, the Europeans knelt before Francis submissively. His Japanese host took the bait. Thinking Francis must in fact be a man of great influence, he granted the priest free reign. Other nobles soon followed.

But despite all his efforts, Francis managed to baptize only a thousand Japanese over the next two and a half years. He was gratified that one among this thousand was a shogun. The shogun in turn would become the first Japanese ever to use what the Church calls "St. Paul's Privilege"—a rule by which a Catholic can legally divorce a non-Catholic in order to marry a Catholic. But all in all, this was small potatoes compared to his landslide successes in India.

Francis knew how eagerly the Japanese took their cues from China. Japanese life and culture was thick with Chinese-born trends and customs, language, arts—and spirituality. Francis knew what he must do. He must baptize all of China.

As it had for years, China kept a strict no-foreigners policy. Caucasians caught entering the country were sentenced to death.

Francis decided to take his chances. Pulling political

strings, he arranged for a Portuguese friend to be appointed ambassador to China. Soon an expedition was under way. With Francis in tow, the Portuguese bore gifts which he thought no emperor could resist. But the party got only as far as western Malaysia before local officials turned it away. Francis was mocked in the streets before the ships sailed back to India.

He did not wait long before trying again. This time, even more desperate, Francis sailed to Shangchwan, an island off the coast near Canton. Portuguese traders sometimes lodged on this island, though only briefly and at high risk. The traders waited here while Chinese boatmen ferried European merchandise back and forth to buyers onshore.

Francis was set on finding a ferryman to carry him across. Some say he caught a fever on board ship even before reaching the island and was carried ashore dead or dying. Other accounts say he landed hale and hearty, but that he failed to find a boatman willing to face the penalties for transporting a white man. Thinking he could change their minds, Francis set up camp. Rain poured through the roof of his hut, and he sickened and died.

HIS BODY WAS buried on the island. Later it was unearthed and taken to Malaysia. There, hailed as incorrupt, it was installed in the first of many churches it would occupy over the next several years. Finally it was taken to Goa, where crowds of converts gathered along with Goa's resident Europeans to adore the exposed corpse. In 1544 a Portuguese woman bent to kiss its foot and sneakily bit off a toe. Refusing to relinquish her prize, she ran off with the toe in her mouth.

In 1614, after some years away from the public eye, Francis's body was exhumed. It is said that the corpse appeared soft, moist and fresh. Its right eye was wide open, and twinkling. At that point, the arm was ceremoniously amputated at the elbow and sent on its way to Rome.

The corpse was entombed and lay unseen for decades before being exhumed again nearly 150 years after Francis's death. At that point, witnesses wrote of its curly hair, red lips—even of two purplish veins standing out on its forehead. Someone pierced the corpse and its blood ran, fluid. The eye was still open.

Requests for relics came in from churches all over the world. So, bit by bit, Francis was dismembered. Half of the left hand went to Cochin, the other half to Malacca. Internal organs were distributed as well. It is unpleasant to think that each new surgery spurted blood.

Braced internally with wires to fill in for the missing viscera, the corpse now lies under glass in Goa's Basilica of Bom Jesus. It is seldom put on public display.

And the arm is in Rome. You wonder who carried it. In what sort of luggage did it travel? A kind of Renaissance valise? Did the courier set it on a chair beside him while he ate?

A FRIEND OF mine was raised in Goa. He has told me that stories about Francis peppered his childhood. The saint's name, his legend, and his image popped up constantly in my friend's Catholic household.

Francis may have baptized tens of thousands in Asia, though later scholars dispute this figure. Hailed as the greatest missionary ever, he certainly altered the continent's spiritual landscape. Preaching in lands about which he knew nothing to people of whom he knew nothing, he battled to uproot the strong faiths that sustained them. Amid his warnings of hellfire, mesmerized by songs and bells, throngs found themselves baptized almost by accident, as if in a dream. If children could be used as pawns, then all the better. By all accounts, Francis loved children. That he believed he was doing all this for their own good may be true. But to a non-Christian—Jews, more than almost anyone else on earth, oppose proselytizing—such a conviction is hard to assimilate. That strangers who are minding their own business, miles and miles away, must be wrested from their faith and converted to one's own seems absurd, a premise dangerous and brutal at worst but pointless at best. It would be laughable if it were not so popular. Francis lived and died for it.

In one letter, Francis urged Portugal's king to let him launch the Inquisition in India. Begun in the thirteenth century, this was a general tribunal set up to punish heretics. Its arrival in India, Francis felt, would rout the Jews and Moslems, and give the stubborn Brahmans their comeuppance. Francis was to miss seeing his wish come true by eight years. By 1567, fifteen years after his death, India's Inquisition was well underway. Nearly 300 Hindu temples were burned down that year, and laws were imposed prohibiting Goans from celebrating Hindu marriages, Hindu funerals, or the festivities they had always held to honor harvests, puberty, birth, eclipses, and the phases of the moon. Goan men were prohibited from wearing their traditional wraparound dhotis. Women's clothing too was regulated. And all Goans over fifteen years of age were compelled under threat of severe penalties to attend church.

A PLACARD IS posted on the marble railing in front of Francis's arm. In Italian it explains how Francis, the first Jesuit missionary, "dedicated ten years to the conversion of India and Japan."

This *braccio*, this arm, the placard says, "baptized thousands and thousands of infidels." A monk kneels before the railing. Three British tourists argue in the dark like restless guests at a slumber party.

"He was bishop of Geneva," one says insistently of Francis. "No no wait, I've got him mixed up with St. Francis de Sales."

"He went to Asia," reads another from the sign.

"That's right," cries the first. He nods. "Now I recall. He didn't persecute them."

"Big of him," snorts the third Briton, who is black.

The first persists. "He let them wear their native costumes." In the silence afterward they shrug and walk away.

A Kitchen Full of Angels

▼▼▼▼▼

ST. ZITA
Church of St. Frediano
Lucca, Italy

dRINKING ESPRESSO IN Lucca's Caffe Elisa I start thinking I could live here. I could disappear quite happily amid the city's ramparts.

Arches catch the morning sun, their yellow stone half-blinding. Awnings flap, the green of rosemary and boats. Steam rises from the coffee cups amid the sound of bright machines, the click of sugar-spoons.

Along the streets, pastry shops opening their doors exhale the heavy smell of slivered almonds. From the Tuscan hills, warm wind sighs down the street. Delicatessens proffer noodles in all colors. They come shaped like wedding rings, ears, vulvas for a joke.

ST. ZITA'S RELICS lie in the church of St. Frediano. Her mummy wears a turquoise satin frock under a white gauze apron that recalls her long career as housemaid in a wealthy house in Lucca.

Corpo incorrotto, says the placard in front of her mummy. But the body begs to differ, its brown feet crumbling. The skin on its crossed hands is curling up like Scotch tape left out in the sun. Still, what can you expect? The corpse has been here more than 700 years.

Propped against glass, the sign insists: *Non imbalsamato*.

ZITA'S MOTHER HAD two favorite phrases. One was "This would please God." The other was "This would displease God." She taught Zita that she must label all her thoughts and actions with one of the two.

At twelve, around the year 1230, Zita went to work for Lucca's wealthy Fatinelli family. She threw herself into her chores. Her mother had taught her that labor could wash away sin. So Zita prayed while working.

Her fellow servants could not abide her. Some called her stupid. Others called her pretentious, bristling at the great show Zita made of her diligence. Some called her sanctimonious, a charge bolstered by Zita's penchant for fasting, and for sleeping on the bare floor.

The other servants blamed her for whatever went wrong. Zita's master and mistress disliked her. Her master was known to have flown into rages, just looking at her. They kept her on, and took to beating her. Zita said she was grateful for this chance to practice obedience, to submit.

SHE LEFT THE house only to perform her master's errands, to attend mass, and to visit fellow churchgoers even poorer than she.

One of Zita's chores was baking bread. She was getting started one morning when urgent word reached her of an emergency at a poor family's home. She left at once to help. Staying away longer than she knew she should, Zita fretted over her undone task. (Another version of the same story says she went to church and lost herself in prayer, forgetting all about the bread.)

After she had gone, the other servants hurried to tell their master and mistress that Zita was AWOL. Hungry for the bread they now deduced was not forthcoming, the Fatinellis thundered to the kitchen.

Its door was closed. They smelled the sweet aroma of bread baking.

They flung open the door to find the kitchen full of angels who were calmly taking pans out of the oven.

THIS INCIDENT CHANGED forever Zita's status in the household. The other servants no longer mocked her. She was put in charge of them all.

Whenever one of them upset the master, Zita groveled at his feet begging his forgiveness on the underling's behalf. Sometimes the whole household watched her fall into a trance as she prayed. Living ascetically in a garret, she would run gladly into rainstorms on the merest of her master's whims.

But all her diligence could not suppress Zita's Robin Hood tendencies. One day in the midst of a famine, she is said to have given the poor her employers' entire hoard of beans. Learning what she had done, her master rushed to his cupboard. Expecting to find it empty, he had a surprise. Beans gleamed up at him, a full supply having miraculously replaced the ones Zita gave away.

As Zita was hurrying out to attend church one cold Christmas Eve, Signore Fatinelli offered to loan her his fur coat, a family heirloom. She acquiesced as he pulled it over her shoulders, warning her all the while to take good care of it.

Approaching the church, she spied a homeless man shivering in the doorway. Without a second thought Zita shrugged off her coat and helped him put it on. It was a loan, she thought, and she would collect it from him after the mass. She went inside. As always, the ritual moved her to tears.

But afterward, the homeless man was nowhere to be seen. Walking home through the freezing streets she knew she had gone too far. What she had done was unforgivable.

Zita was right. As she entered the house without his coat the master raged at her like never before. But then over the sound of his shouts they heard a knock at the door.

It was the homeless man. He had come to give Zita back the cloak.

As the story made its way through Lucca afterward, everyone began saying the man was obviously an angel in disguise. On a bitter day, Zita had clothed an angel. That is why to this day the church of St. Frediano's door is called the Angel Portal.

ZITA'S LEGEND, ABSORBED in one sitting, has a way of making you feel as if you've just eaten an entire box of Mystic Mints. All saints' legends include their share of supernatural happenings: visions, stigmata, healings, bilocation. But the phenomena surrounding Zita is entirely of the goody-goody sort, pounding home with relentless heavy-handedness the saint's persona as a simple, sweet servant with a heart of gold. If her biographers are to be believed—beginning with the first, whose book appeared 400 years after Zita's death, in 1688—then Zita lived to serve. Hers is a knee-jerk goodness. As if her servility around the house was not enough (a servility rewarded frequently, in her early years at least, with beatings), she also served the poor. This she did with a singlemindedness that only makes her character appear all the more one-dimensional. The rare occasions on which we glimpse conflict in Zita's story occur when she sparks her master's ire. But then Fatinelli, too, takes on a cookie-cutter quality. As a rich man with a short fuse, he serves as the perfect foil for this woman whose relentless goodness makes her appear almost mesmerized.

Like other saints such as Maria Goretti, Zita is painted for us in broad strokes and primary colors with all the subtlety of a billboard. A child might take Zita's story as it comes, but the more inquisitive reader cannot help but feel hoodwinked, and wonder. Did Zita weep when Fatinelli beat her? Did she bridle in the cold that Christmas Eve, rushing home coatless?

I crave details to match her corpse. That, at least, is frank. Crumbling and clad in aqua blue, her mummy proves Zita was flesh and blood.

JUST INSIDE THE Angel Portal, a worker in a white smock smeared with paint is standing on a ladder. Hair tied back with a ribbon, she smacks bubble gum while repairing the wall. Wearing designer jeans under her smock, she dabs at the wet plaster with a fingertip. Nearby, the pipe-organ soars ceilingward. That such a huge instrument should ever be silent is almost frightening. Through a tiny stained-glass window, light spills from the summer sky onto the floor.

The church is large yet unintimidating, its marble walls

speckled like nougat. In the transept a small girl marches flat-footed in a yellow sunsuit. Her feet make slapping sounds. She prattles and her voice wells up, amplified. She shrieks with pleasure just to hear. These are acoustics made for hymns, for organs, and for little girls discovering how large a space they occupy in the world.

I'm thinking I could live here.

Zita's glass case forms the centerpiece of a marble chapel. The casket containing the mummy is not poised up high at the top of any steps or encrusted with silver angels or obscured behind a lattice. As one of Europe's most accessible and visitor-friendly mummies, it invites intimate and unencumbered inspection. Children and legless pilgrims can get as close to it as they desire.

Against the soapy glint of white sateen the mummy lies with its arms crossed, as if waiting with endless patience. Ravaged heels rest on a brocade pillow trimmed in gold. Propped on a matching cushion, the mummy's head has the color and tautness of a teabag just plucked from the cup. Framed with a white gauze veil and pale pink artificial roses, Zita's darkened skin pulls taut over wide cheekbones and a trowel of a chin. The years have stolen Zita's lips.

Eyes crushed, nose hooked, Zita has her mouth open, the way grandmothers sometimes sleep.

SHE DIED AT sixty. After visiting this church every day of her adult life, in April 1278 she had what was called a happy death. And at the moment she breathed her last, they say the church bell began ringing by itself. Entombed here though not, at first, on display, Zita's newly deceased body immediately attracted its own cult of devotees. As the years passed—and the housemaid would not be canonized until more than four centuries after her death—she became increasingly popular. As far away as England, where her name was spelled as Citha and Sita, church walls and stained-glass windows depict scenes from Zita's story.

THAT STORY URGES selfless obedience. But it carries another message that no doubt accounts for some of its widespread appeal.

Zita was neither a nun nor a noble. Any volume of saints' lives reveals how many were one or the other or even, before they died, both. Elizabeth, Ignatius, Francis Xavier, and many more were born in castles. Embracing poverty was, for them, rebellion. The depth of their sacrifice, of what they gave up, just enhances the drama. We would likely balk at making the same choice. Then again few of us will ever reach the fortunate position from which to make it. The celebrity of saints who were clerics or rich kids is unreachable. Who could relate?

Yet Zita was born poor. And poor she stayed. Nor did she commit herself to the rarefied realm of a convent but scrubbed floors and shopped in the market. Stripping away the few comforts to which she was entitled, she fasted and slept on the floor. Zita's story offers the promise that *anyone* can hope for sainthood—provided he or she is very, *very* good.

MORE THAN 300 years after her death, Zita's remains were exhumed. Found well-preserved, they were declared incorrupt and set out on display. Today the "Little Maid of Lucca," also known as the "Little Cook of Lucca," is the patron saint of housewives and domestics. It is also said that she can help you find lost keys, if St. Anthony disappoints.

Surrounding her body in the chapel is a series of seventeenth-century paintings. In one, Zita gives bread to a beggar.

Another depicts the miracle of the beans. Another shows Zita caught in the act of swiping bread from her master's house with which she plans to feed the poor. According to this legend—which recurs in the stories of other goody-two-shoes female saints including Germaine Cousin—Fatinelli demands to see what Zita is hiding. When she unbundles her apron it is not bread that tumbles out but flowers.

Every year on Zita's deathday, April 27, Lucca holds a festival, filling its piazza with spring flowers. Hundreds come to touch the saint.

A SCOTS COUPLE enters the chapel wearing hiking boots whose rubber soles make violent chirps against the fresh-scrubbed floor.

"Ye shouldna have eaten it then," the white-haired man is admonishing his wife, nudging her with what looks like a ski pole but is a walking stick.

"I feel poorly," she says.

"So that's actually a body," cries the man, pressing his face up to the casket.

"Yes," his wife says. "I feel poorly."

"I don't think I'd want to be shown after I was dead," says the man but pronounces it *deed*.

"Ye wouldna last that long," says his wife. She sinks into a pew and unfastens her knapsack. "Well maybe ye would."

Until I Am Nailed

▼▼▼▼▼

St. Gemma Galgani
Sanctuary of St. Gemma
Lucca, Italy

In a trash can in Lucca are pages torn from a comic book. I snatch them out to read on a bench in an empty piazza where no one will see. The comic is an Italian edition of a Japanese *manga*—not the kiddie kind like *Sailor Moon*, with big-eyed princesses and kitten robots, but the erotic kind. A man is peering at a woman's anus. Translated from Japanese, the caption reads in Italian, "You want me to put my tongue in THERE??!!"

"*Si,*" she says.

The woman's genitals are shown in great detail, though for

Italian readers the man's crotch has been obscured with blocks of Zip-a-tone.

The woman screams, "I'm com-i-i-i-n-n-ng," in Italian.

Sweat leaps, gleaming, from her partner's face.

"You nymphomaniac," he says.

Two schoolgirls are crossing the piazza eating candy and shoving one another. One wears a backpack slung over her shoulder emblazoned with the single word *College*. Her friend's bears a picture of a popeyed face with the slogan *Jolly Black*.

INSIDE THE SANCTUARY of Santa Gemma, where Gemma Galgani's relics lie entombed, the ultramodern architecture is white and blockish as if carved from Camay soap. Translucent marble slabs, striped like steak, are set into the walls in place of stained-glass windows. Light streams through the stripes that look like fat.

Over the altar is a massive painting in a modern style. It does not show the saint as any vain young woman would desire to look. Gemma kneels, chicken-necked, raising her arms. Stigmata stains her hands bright red. The angel who is watching has no nose. Christ hangs suspended on the cross. His wounded breast spurts blood, a scarlet jet that arcs suggestively over the young saint's head.

The tomb that hides her corpse is streamlined, sleek, in contrast with cheap pots of pink and yellow roses that a steady stream of visitors has left. Above it all a white dome looms, unpainted, like a planetarium.

Keep silent, warns a sign.

A FLUORESCENT LIGHT burns in the sanctuary's gift shop. The scent of hair spray rises as a party of female pilgrims darts back and forth. On the glass counter, a cardboard box is filling steadily with souvenirs they wish to buy. Bumping into one another in their excitement they tap the glass case with manicured fingernails whose frosted polish flatters the women's honey-brown skin. Two nuns wait on them. One wears Buddy Holly glasses. Asking in shattered English for a closer look at what they see inside the case, the shoppers fondle figurines and necklaces and metal frames the size of postage stamps containing tiny photographs of Gemma.

Her hair is dark, but thin from illness. Parted starkly in the middle as befits a fin-de-siecle girl, it frames a face from which I cannot look away.

She is the weirdest girl in school.

She stares into the lens coolly indulgent, with a brilliance that in certain lights could pass for crazy.

GEMMA WAS A very little girl the first time she heard what she thought was God addressing her one day in church. He asked her to give him her mother. Musing over the prospect of her mother's death, she shuddered.

"Only," Gemma dickered, "if you take me too."

God scolded her, called her unwilling. In her autobiography, Gemma would write that she realized even then there was no point arguing. Her fate was sealed. Her mother caught TB and died. Gemma was eight.

Soon afterward she begged to take her first communion. "Give me Jesus," she cajoled the nuns. "Give him to me. I long for him."

"I cannot express," she later wrote of that communion, "what passed between myself and Jesus."

AFTER WINNING A citywide scholastic contest, Gemma attended the awards ceremony with her father. She wore her best outfit, including a gold watch. In the middle of the ceremony she heard the sonorous voice of what could only be her guardian angel.

How dare she wear jewelry, the angel snorted. The only accessory befitting a bride of the crucified Christ, the angel declared, is a crown of thorns.

Gemma resolved not to wear ornaments ever again, nor to speak of them. Chastened, she "asked Jesus to let me suffer." Soon afterward her foot began to ache. Stemming from a growth on the bone, her condition grew worse and finally required surgery.

She was eighteen when, on Christmas Day, she believed she heard Jesus commanding that she consecrate her virginity to him. She was only too willing, feeling ecstatic at the offer and "like I was in heaven."

Her mother's medical bills had left her family poor. Now Gemma's father developed throat cancer and died as well, leaving his children destitute. Gemma would later remember creditors raiding her home soon after her father's death, picking it clean, snatching coins from her pockets.

She was sent to live with a married aunt. There she attracted not one but two suitors. Gemma fled.

A spinal condition blossomed which made it difficult for Gemma to walk. She saw this as a God-given opportunity to suffer as Jesus had, and firmly refused to see any doctors. By the time she relented, she had lost the use of her legs.

Inflammation along the vertebrae had led to an abscess that climbed upward toward her skull. Paralyzed and tormented with headaches, she lay in bed one evening and overheard the physicians telling one another that she would not last the night.

Gemma began praying in earnest to Gabriel of Our Lady of Sorrows, a young Italian priest and future saint who had died of tuberculosis sixteen years before she was born. She would later write of how Gabriel came to her sickbed, where he caressed her and called her "sister." Detaching the emblem from his cassock he pressed it to her breast and let her hold it and kiss it.

When they saw that she would live, Gemma's doctors decided to operate. The surgery entailed cauterizations along the spine, but Gemma refused anesthetics.

A month after her doctors had said she would die, Gemma got out of bed and walked.

She longed to join a local convent. The illness had left her temporarily bald, and she wore a heavy metal back-brace. This and her poverty were the nuns' reasons for turning her away. She was on her own.

ONE SPRING DAY, Gemma felt faint. She hurried to lock the door of her room. Jesus appeared before her, as she would later write, bleeding vigorously. Pressing her forehead to the floor for what turned out to be hours, she was terrified to look straight at the apparition. But she was sure she heard Jesus say, "Love me!"

One Thursday a few months later, she had a vision of Mary. Jesus loved Gemma very much, the Virgin said. Then as if at the mention of his name, Christ appeared. His five wounds were not bleeding but shooting fire. Flames leaped out to lick the corresponding spots on Gemma's body. As they touched her, searing pain tore through her hands, feet, and side. For the next few hours, Gemma knelt in such agony that the Virgin had to keep propping her up, so that Gemma did not tip over onto the floor.

Afterward, when Mary and Jesus had vanished, Gemma rose to find open sores in her flesh, all oozing blood. The stigmata were still seeping the next morning as she dressed for church. Gloves did little to hide the gore.

Her wounds lasted until the next afternoon, then disappeared. The following Thursday they opened again and bled. Again they bled for a day. Every week, the same thing happened: Gemma's wounds bled from Thursday until Friday.

As news of her stigmata spread, a priest came to examine them. He wrote that they began as mere red marks. The epidermis ripped gradually until rounded holes resembling puncture wounds appeared in her palms. Slits opened on the backs of her hands. Blood ran. By Friday evening they bled no more, the priest noted. The holes in her hands sealed themselves, though pale marks showed where they had been.

KNOWING HOW POOR she was, a family invited Gemma to live with them. Like nearly everyone in town, the Gianninis had heard of her stigmata and the other phenomena, and it intrigued them. Ushering her into their home, they hoped to glimpse some of what brought Gemma her curious celebrity.

Sharing a bedroom with the family's matriarch, Gemma adopted a new daily routine. Domestic chores and communal meals she interspersed with physical penances. Free to do as she liked, she began exchanging letters with a Roman priest. He urged her to keep a diary and then, noting her eloquence, to write an autobiography. Dozens of letters streamed back and forth between the pair: Gemma insisted that many of these were carried not by the postal service, as she had not mailed them, but by an angel.

To the Gianninis she spoke little. Before her morning visits to church she said nothing at all. At mealtimes she took her accustomed place at the table, her back to the family's dining room shrine with its large wooden crucifix. Its Jesus

▼▼▼▼▼

was the size of a snowshoe, with painted blood coursing over a downcast face. A carved loincloth hid very little skin. Gemma was fond of kissing the figure's painted wounds.

Throughout the day, she meditated on the crucifixion. When she felt a vision coming on, she scurried to her room.

Knowing their cue, the Giannini women took to following her. Gemma was oblivious, already half in trance as Cecilia, Giustina, Eufemia, and Annetta Giannini slipped into the room behind her. They watched as Gemma fell onto the bed or into the armchair, speaking loudly and in an odd voice to unseen figures she addressed as Jesus, Mary, or an angel.

Pencils in hand, the Giannini women wrote down everything they saw during Gemma's daily trances. Once they went so far as to take a photograph. It shows Gemma's face deathly pale, her lips pursed, her eyes fixed on something so high above her head as to display mostly their whites. Whenever they saw that she was coming back to her senses, the spies hurried away.

SOMETIMES GEMMA'S SUPERNATURAL episodes took a totally different direction. She went wild. Later claiming that demons led her to it, she raged around the house desecrating religious items. Once she shattered a rosary. Another time she spat fiercely on the dining room crucifix. She blamed demons for setting fire to the manuscript she was writing. And she blamed them for what happened one day in the Gianninis' garden, when sensual longings so consumed her that Gemma rushed to extinguish them in the icy water of the well.

IN THE SPRING of 1902, she was twenty-four. The Gianninis watched helplessly as her ill health returned. This time Gemma would not recover. As she lay in bed she begged her companions not to leave her "until I am nailed to the cross.

"I have to be crucified," she said, "with Jesus."
Flinging her arms out to the sides, she died.

THOUGH HER TEACHERS later reported that Gemma excelled at many subjects, religious studies was her favorite. In that case she must have read about her compatriots Catherine of Siena and Catherine de' Ricci: In nearly identical visions, centuries earlier, both saw Jesus pledging his love to them. Probably Gemma also knew of France's Marguerite Marie Alacoque, who claimed Christ had torn out his flaming heart for her alone to see.

Many female saints spoke of meeting Jesus amid imagery that can hardly fail to arouse: heat, embraces, beams of intense light that shot from his body to theirs to penetrate the flesh. (Such claims raised more than a few eyebrows. Marguerite Marie's fellow nuns disliked her intensely.) Among the best known of these visionaries is Teresa of Ávila, who wrote of an angel who approached her with a long flaming dart:

"I felt him thrust it several times through my heart in such a way that it passed through my very bowels. And when he drew it out . . . left me wholly on fire."

In Rome, Bernini's arguably orgasmic *The Ecstasy of St. Teresa* titillates sightseers.

Gemma and the others were deeply religious women. But they were *women*. Living in a time and place that flatly denied their desire, they had no dance clubs at their disposal, no tube tops with which to express themselves, no erotic manga. One was led to believe that any such longings were Satan's work. In that world, one did not flirt with the boy who ran the fruit stall. What's a girl to do?

Within their midst—everywhere, and certainly on every bedroom wall—was the crucifix. In a world without Chippendale's, every woman was greeted wherever she went by the sight of a near-naked man. She was exhorted to love him. Nuns became his brides. Artists, also chastened to channel all their inspiration into Christian subjects, lavished their attention on his thighs, flat belly, and the nipples on his chest, his face contorted with passion. That Jesus is pierced and that he is famous only tightens the ratchet. My British friend who attended Catholic schools remembers a nun flushing red and turning hoarse, her monologue dissolving into sharp explosive gasps as she described the crucifixion to a classroom full of puzzled students.

And the Gianninis' crucifix, still on display as the house is open to visitors, is in some lights attractive indeed.

IMMEDIATELY AFTER GEMMA'S death, visitors began lining up to gaze at her emaciated corpse. Already an object of veneration, it was buried along with a copy of Gemma's memoir.

But the corpse's continued popularity led to its exhumation later that spring. Talk of beatification was afoot. As part of the procedure, surgeons opened Gemma's chest and extracted her heart. Witnesses reported that it emerged moist and plump, as if cut from a living body. Under the surgeons' knives, it spurted blood all over the table.

Gemma was reburied. This time a monument, financed by Gemma's pen pal the Roman priest, was erected to set her grave apart from the ordinary ones all around it. More pilgrims started arriving than ever. By the time Gemma was canonized in 1940, her autobiography had been published to popular acclaim. Fifteen years later, her relics resided in the angular white sanctuary where they are enshrined to this day.

THE STREET IN Lucca on which she lived as a child has been renamed via Santa Gemma. Elsewhere in town the

Until I Am Nailed

▼▼▼▼▼

Giannini house and garden are preserved as they were when Gemma lodged there. Visitors tour the room where she had her visions, the bedroom she shared with Cecilia Giannini. Against striped wallpaper stand a small white-covered bed and the matriarch's four-poster. On a shelf is a statuette of the Madonna, a gauze veil flowing from its spiky crown nearly to its feet, which Gemma's mother gave her before dying. The crucifix hangs in its crimson-lined shrine beside the dining table.

Photographs of the saint and figures important to her are scattered around the house's pastel walls. They peer at visitors from above overstuffed chairs and stout desks. The bureau is shown from which, as Gemma claimed, the angel collected her outgoing mail. From the garden, where the well recalls Gemma's struggle against her senses, you can see the upstairs window behind which she died.

AT THE SANCTUARY, a room adjoining the gift shop is lined with shelves displaying Gemma's personal effects. Slippers and socks rest under the harsh light. Pages from her diary reveal a rapid, confident cursive script. One page on display is singed—Gemma said a demon did it.

Her undershirt, her table napkin, cup and saucer, spoon, and bedsheet fill the shelves. A sign explains that the pair of white doves, now stuffed and mounted, took part in Gemma's canonization ceremony in 1940. Another shelf, not far from her folded handkerchief, holds a black-handled whip. This, too, was Gemma's. She used it on herself.

IN THE GIFT shop, the women pilgrims are filling their box with souvenirs.

Their husbands wait along the wall on folding chairs. They share the women's honey-brown complexions. One has a gap between his front teeth. He wears a Cybex baseball cap and a T-shirt that reads *Harley-Davidson: The Legend Rides.* Between his feet rests a shopping bag.

He says they are all Indonesians now living in Holland. After emigrating to Europe, he says, they learned about Gemma.

"All her life, she was so sick," he says of the saint, gazing across the room at her picture, replicated over and over. "So maybe she can help if you have a cyst," he says and shrugs, as if cysts are only to be expected, "or some other sickness."

He looks up at one of the women beside the counter. Blue stretch pants and a San Francisco 49ers sweatshirt strain across her large hips.

"This woman is very spiritual," says the man, who may or may not be her husband. "She is very interested in St. Gemma."

The box on the counter is piled high with framed icons in which Gemma's large eyes and white face are given the stylized Russian treatment. The women are buying stacks of holy cards printed with prayers addressed to Gemma. The one in the 49ers sweatshirt hefts a handful of silvery Gemma medals before letting them clatter gently into the box. A rosary made of sky-blue plastic beads dangles over the flap.

To Wear His Ring

▼▼▼▼

St. Catherine de' Ricci
*Basilica of St. Vincent Ferrer and St. Catherine de' Ricci
Prato, Italy*

a GYPSY GIRL of about eleven wearing tight rainbow-striped bell bottoms stands in my way. Then she hops down into the gutter and squats, urinating through the seat of her trousers. A pool forms between her shoes, sparkling in the summer sun, collecting silt. Her face is blank, the black strings of her hair hang down her cheeks. Her two small sisters on the sidewalk jump around, enclosing me. They wave pieces of cardboard in my face. I stand patiently like a farm animal. They pluck at the sleeve of my T-shirt, poke my collarbone, my purse. The cardboard makes a whirring sound.

The girls make gurgling noises in their throats. The hiss of urine resounds in the street.

This is the wrecked allure of Italy. Whether you find it on the first day of your visit or the last is merely chance.

IN PISA'S PIZZA bar called On the Road the clerk follows my eyes past unappealing plates of sandwiches on white sliced bread. His frigid pizzas are as thin as matzah in their dotage, with a mucous red sauce flicked over them lightly. Following my eyes the clerk clucks, *Pizza, pizza* in a grieving voice. A tourist in the corner wears a baseball cap and khaki shorts and he is talking on the public phone.

"Mom, I'm in Pisa."

Standing near him is a girl in matching shorts and matching cap, her hair pulled tightly back.

"Florence was beautiful," the young man shouts. He draws a curve across the air with one hand as if to describe a dome, as if his mother in the States can see.

"Sharon and I were both in *tears.*" He rubs his eyes.

"We're going on a tour tomorrow—where?" He pokes the girl.

She blinks. "Capri."

"That's right, Mom," shouts the man. "Capri."

ON THE STREET leading to the Leaning Tower, African vendors are selling belts with big square metal buckles. They are all selling the same selection of belts. Clutching handfuls of belts which dangle from their fists like disembodied tongues they ply the crowd, accosting tourists. It is not the sort of situation in which you would regularly think of buying belts. As if, right here, you would suddenly think: *I say, my pants are just too loose.*

Meanwhile other vendors, most of them Chinese, are selling

wind-up plastic soldiers. Wearing camouflage, the soldiers crawl across the pavement jerkily upon their knees and elbows, squeaking. They bump into each other, clacking softly, head to hip, until the vendors reach across and separate them.

A GRAFFITO IN the station says *Kurt Kobain Rest in Pis.*

PRATO IS OFF the tourist track. I board the train amid the hubbub of Pisa and Florence thinking I will never flee these legions of my countrymen and those who prey on them. But minutes later, the scenery outside the window turns to countryside. The tile roofs bake under the sun. Swinging a basket an old woman strolls right up the middle of a village street, alone. The train whisks past abandoned villas. Built too near the track, perhaps, they stand imploding like spoiled squash.

Out in the fields, fallen tomatoes shine amid the ruin of their vines, like battle dead.

THEN PRATO RISES from the plain. Ringed by textile factories, it has been called the Manchester of Italy. Its name does not appear in all the guidebooks. Its plain park fronting the station is a far cry from the crowded ones in Pisa. On its concrete walkways, factory workers enjoy their days off. Most are Chinese men playing with babies. Perhaps these are the husbands of those women selling toy soldiers half an hour away.

The Old Town lies on the far side of a bustling modern district where the Chinese shop for socks and cake.

IN THE OLD Town, the Basilica of St. Vincent Ferrer and St. Catherine de' Ricci has its name chiseled high along the outside wall. It is a long name that goes on and on, making the white stone church look even smaller than it is. If any tourists reach Prato they will not likely reach the basilica. The town's more famous church is its cathedral. In the Middle Ages it was famous for a relic.

Thomas the Apostle—Doubting Thomas—refused to believe that Mary had entered bodily into heaven. Demanding that her tomb be opened, Thomas found it empty except for white lilies and roses. He gazed heavenward and saw the Virgin smiling down at him indulgently. The legend says that she untied her sash and threw it down to him as proof. A cloth said to be Mary's sash was enshrined in Prato's cathedral, to the endless joy of pilgrims. It's gone now.

BUT IN THE basilica with its long name, Catherine de' Ricci's mummy wears a crown. Its silver whorls are studded with red gems arranged in flower shapes—the kind of crown that invades schoolgirls' dreams.

Catherine's black robe is trimmed in heavy lace. The white gown underneath gives off a pearly sheen.

Against all this, her face with its prominent nose is nearly black. It looks quite soft, like overripe bananas. She looks younger than the saint was when she died at sixty-seven in 1590. Death becomes her. Underneath the mummy, like a thin divan, a fine white cushion is embellished with golden flourishes, a Renaissance design. It is the shining cloth of dreams.

Catherine, dressed in finery, despised her flesh.

PROTRUDING FROM THE basilica's walls, above the altar on which Catherine's mummy lies in its glass case, are pure white marble sculptures. Life-size, they loom overhead evoking scenes from Catherine's visions. Captions run beneath in gilded letters.

We see Catherine on her knees. She reaches up to kiss Christ's hand while he's in agony. He grimaces, perhaps thinking: Don't *bother* me already.

In another scene, Catherine embraces Christ while he hangs on the cross. It is an awkward pose, for he is nailed. She half cradles, half lifts his helpless body.

In another, Christ is giving her an engagement ring. Her joy belies the stark cut of her habit. *Amore perfetto*, reads the caption: Perfect love. Her white hand rises, winglike, toward her suitor.

BORN IN FLORENCE in 1522 into a very old and powerful family of bankers and merchants, Catherine was originally named Alessandra. The family acknowledged that whenever Alessandra was nowhere to be found, she was off by herself in some secret corner, kneeling and praying the way other little girls sneak off to write in their diaries.

When she was six, Alessandra went to live in a nearby convent where her aunt was a nun. When after a year or so her father brought her home, Alessandra begged him to let her become a nun. She could not bear the clatter of the outside world.

She was fourteen when she visited Prato, where her uncle was a priest connected with the Convent of St. Vincent.

The convent had been founded not long before by a small group of women who were devoted followers of the radical Florentine monk Girolamo Savonarola. Alessandra adored him.

AT ST. MARK'S cathedral in Florence, Savonarola preached terrifying sermons. He told his listeners he'd had a vision of the near future: God was at hand, showing mercy to believers while slicing sinners to ribbons. Worldly pleasures must be denounced at once in order to win God's mercy, Savonarola urged. Famine, bloodshed, and plague were on their way.

His listeners ate it up. When Savonarola traveled to nearby towns including Prato, enthusiastic crowds hung on his every word.

Exercising his influence, he instituted laws ensuring that Florence's poor were fed. At his urging, taxes affecting the lower classes were reduced. Business hours were increased to create jobs for the unemployed.

Every year, the carnival preceding Lent sparked wild revelry throughout the city. Savonarola loathed it. In 1497, he staged an alternative carnival that featured dancing monks garlanded in flowers. In the original "bonfire of the vanities," party masks and fancy-dress costumes were piled up and burned in a piazza. Also thrown into the flames were women's cosmetics, artworks, and books that Savonarola deemed indecent. He held the city in the palm of his hand. One year later, the tides had changed and he was executed.

DELIGHTED TO FIND a convent that bore Savonarola's stamp, Alessandra took the veil—and, with it, the name Catherine.

She had been performing physical penances for years, hurting herself. Now as a new nun, the pain was augmented by a mysterious lingering illness. The medicines she took only seemed to make her sicker.

Her own pain infused Catherine's absorption with the crucifixion. Dwelling on every detail of Christ's misery, she would spend hours at a time meditating on it. When after two years her illness retreated, Catherine adopted her harshest penitential regime yet. It was a way to maintain the level of pain to which she had become accustomed. She took to flagellating herself. Under her habit, a sharp iron chain bit into her flesh. She forced herself to survive two or three days of every week on a diet of bread and water only. Some days she let herself eat nothing at all.

The other nuns heard Catherine praying that she might "die" to her senses: in other words, not to heed them. She begged God to control her heart and mind, her thoughts, her speech and her preferences. In this way, she hoped, any choices she made would not be really hers.

For all her professed desire to be anonymous, passive, to relinquish her thoughts, Catherine had a funny tendency to make herself the center of attention.

She was twenty when she announced that she had received the stigmata.

Witnesses who investigated Catherine's claims have left mixed reports. Some say they saw her hands pierced clear through and streaming with blood. Others say her hands and feet were uninjured but gave off a brilliant light. Others say they saw what looked like scars.

That same year, she fell into a trance. As she later described it, she saw while in trance all of Christ's agonies, and then the crucifixion itself.

Soon afterward, on Easter Sunday, another vision followed. Catherine saw Christ sliding a ring off his finger and then easing it onto hers. It was a gold ring set with a diamond—proof, Catherine felt, that Christ had personally chosen her as his fiancée. Afterward, as long as she lived, she claimed she still wore the ring on her finger. She insisted that it was there, its white stone sparkling. No one else could see the ring, although some claimed the base of Catherine's finger was swollen and inflamed.

One Thursday she fell into a trance and had, again, her detailed vision of the crucifixion. It was epic, and Catherine remained in trance from noon that day until 4:00 P.M. on Friday. The following Thursday it happened again, and then the next. Word soon spread of Catherine's weekly "Ecstasy of the Passion." Crowds would arrive to watch her spend the long hours shifting from one grotesque pose to another, shouting out loud, her face a mask of pain.

The weekly drama continued for twelve years.

When she was not in trance, Catherine worked as the convent's abbess. Also she tended the sick, selecting the most repugnant duties and performing them all on her knees.

I HAVE ENTERED Prato's basilica to find a service in session. But no priest is apparent. Seated in the pews are a handful of elderly women wearing baggy cardigans over their faded polyester dresses. Grocery baskets trailing spinach and carrot tops rest beside their feet. One old man wearing a tan windbreaker and another in a red sweatshirt are leading a call-and-response that has a cozy quality as they all say: *Mother of this. Mother of that.* Their voices sound like cellophane but still hypnotic as if all these grandmothers are singing lullabies. *Queen of this. Queen of that.*

The service continues as we all sit facing Catherine's mummy. The congregation stands, then kneels, then stands up facing her glass case. Brown feet snug in silver shoes, she is the guest of honor.

WITH HER LIFELONG commitment to self-mutilation, begun when she was a young girl, Catherine exemplifies a whole genre of saints—most of them female. They share a penchant for childhood prayer, and childhood penances such as sleeping on cold castle floors. She trains herself to withstand yet more pain: hair shirts, the whip, no food.

As she grows, the saint cares for the sick. Often this means proselytizing individuals who are too weak to protest, too ill to ignore intimations of heaven and hell. It was not nursing as we know it. Part of the appeal lay in performing nauseous chores: swabbing the patients' running sores, scrubbing their fetid linens. While kindness is to be commended, these saints found in such tasks a way to punish their own senses, perhaps even die.

Sometimes this type of saint—as Catherine did—suffers from chronic illness too. In legend after legend these saints not only endure their agony but welcome it.

Visions ensue.

Young women tend to find themselves seized, now and then, by strong urges and strange impulses. To them, it feels as if the world has jumped completely off its axis. Catherine lived at a time when convents were the only outlet for a girl who felt and acted oddly. And she flourished in a structure that not only praised her odd behaviors but rewarded them with names. Starving is "fasting." Whips are "disciplines." Self-mutilation is "penitence." Suicidal tendencies are channeled into longings for martyrdom, such as those that inspired Thérèse of Lisieux. Erotic daydreams, as in the story of Gemma Galgani, are "demonic temptations." Altered states and what you might call hallucinations are "visions" and "ecstasies."

Born later, Catherine may have pierced her tongue, been a chain-smoking performance artist, been prescribed antipsychotic medications, and wound up in an eating-disorders clinic.

THE HOLY CARDS lying in a pile on a table near the church's door include a photograph showing the relics. In the photograph, Catherine's skin looks paler than it really is.

After the service, the old ladies stand and rub their legs through opaque stockings. Walking stiffly to the altar they reach out and touch the glass.

"*Chiuso*," says the man in the beige windbreaker, jingling a key. The church is closed.

Well Enough Alone

▼▼▼▼▼

ST. DOMINIC AND BLESSED JAMES OF ULM
Basilica of St. Dominic
Bologna, Italy

In front of a university classroom building on the campus in the middle of Bologna, a load of trash is waiting for the collector. Among the debris is an open shoebox holding two headless dolls. All that is left of a Barbie and Ken, they are hard and pink and pale, the wrong complexion for this climate. In their broken beauty they are relics too, holy perhaps to someone, martyred for what college prank or art-class project?

A few blocks away, outside the church of St. Dominic, a man in a starched business shirt with a tie is standing beside a fountain, holding hands with his dog. The dog is a golden retriever, perched on the fountain's stone rim. The man's face is composed until he sees I am watching him. Then his eyes dart back and forth between the dog and me, as if to say *What are you looking at,* as if begging the dog to please forbear this infidel.

BEHIND ITS ROMANESQUE façade, the church's interior stretches far into the distance. Pilgrims sign a guest book near the door, signing themselves as residents of Brazil, Norway, Los Angeles.

Dominic's marble tomb towers ceilingward, like a sandcastle that some child on a fine white sand shore built taller and taller in an effort to see at what point it would tumble. The coterie of sculptors who contributed to its complex array of chiseled images includes Michelangelo. Begun, like the church itself, soon after Dominic's death in 1221, it is adorned with scenes from his life and legend, based largely on the firsthand memories of those who were in a position to know.

In one scene, he restores to life a boy who has fallen— fatally, it was thought—from a horse. In another, he casts his books into a fire together with heretics' books—on a dare, to see whose will survive the flames and whose will burn.

YOU MIGHT SAY Dominic, a Spanish-born priest said to have been irresistibly attractive, is to be praised as a wonderful teacher. You might hum along with Canada's Singing Nun, Sister Sourire, whose 1963 hit "Dominique" lauds the saint's simplicity, his miracles, the fact that God was on his side.

Then again, you might say he helped start the Spanish Inquisition.

A heretical sect called the Cathars had its headquarters in Toulouse but thrived, as the twelfth century melted into the thirteenth, throughout the south of France. Also called the Albigensians after the French town of Albi, another of their strongholds, its followers embraced a cryptic set of beliefs. The first was that *two* gods hold sway: one good and one evil. Constantly at one another's throats, both gods are eternal, though the good one is preferable. The evil god—but a god nonetheless—is Satan himself. During a heavenly battle long ago, Satan incited hosts of angels to join him. Banished from heaven upon their defeat, these rebel angels fell to earth and were imprisoned in human bodies. This, as the Cathars would have it, is how our race began. And thus, they felt, the Earth is Satan's.

To die without accepting the good god would damn a soul to reincarnation. The soul would move on miserably to occupy yet another fleshly jail, human or even animal.

For the Cathars, sex was vile. It was to be avoided. Every child and every animal, they thought, was tainted even before birth by intercourse's poison.

In other words, life is hell.

GAINING NEW ADHERENTS all the time, Cathars fasted three days a week and observed three different Lents every year. Not quite vegetarians, they shunned all meat on the principle that any animal might be a reincarnated soul—though they ate fish, wrongly believing them to give birth in the water *sans* intercourse.

Believers were schooled to revere with absolute obedience a priesthood whose members called themselves the Perfect. As per the First Commandment, the Perfect scrupulously refrained from killing live creatures. They broke all ties with their blood relations. Even more austere than ordinary Cathars, the Perfect were vegans on the principle that cheese, eggs, and milk are all innately sexual substances.

Well Enough Alone

▼▼▼▼▼

❖

FIRST SURFACING IN France around 1020, Catharism reached France via trade routes from Eastern Europe. As its popularity soared throughout the region, the sect found followers and even supporters among the ruling class. Protected by noblemen, and loyal to the Perfect while disdaining Catholic clergy, Cathars presented a clear threat to the pope.

Who knows what would have happened if Innocent III had left the Cathars alone? Their tenets, while unappetizing, were anything but violent.

Dominic accompanied his bishop to Cathar country in 1206. As yet, suspected heretics were punished with excommunication at the very worst. Armed with books and rhetoric, the clever and confident Dominic set out to argue the heretics out of their beliefs.

As the Singing Nun lilts: "with Our Father, he fought against the Albigensians."

They paid him no mind, preferring their own sexless clerics and self-inflicted punishments to his.

When after three years Dominic's mission had proven a failure, the pope ordered an anti-Cathar crusade. As the sect clamored for protection from local nobles in whom it had come to trust, the crusade turned into a bloody civil war. Financed by the Church, armies from northern France charged into the south, massacring heretics. In the town of Béziers where he had come to wipe out a suspected pocket of Cathars, commander Simon de Montfort ordered his army to kill every man, woman, and child they found, regardless of who might or might not be a heretic.

His battle cry, quoted countless times since then, was, "Kill them all. Let God sort them out."

After five years of attacks, the Church had not entirely won. Cathar strongholds dissolved, and Cathars went into hiding. They met in secret, deep in the mountains. Still, the sect lived on.

THROUGHOUT THE REST of that century and part of the next, heretics came under constant attack. The Church began punishing laypersons who were even suspected of sympathizing with the Cathars.

The Inquisition was under way.

Determined to finish what he had begun, Dominic founded a priestly brotherhood dedicated to converting heretics. He established a headquarters in Toulouse. By 1216, his Dominicans were fanning out into France, Spain, and Italy with a vengeance.

Not long after Dominic died in Bologna, a death penalty was declared for heretics throughout Germany and France. In 1231, Dominicans officially took charge of the Inquisition. Two hundred years later, Dominic's home country was a land of religious fanatics. Tomás de Torquemada, Spain's Grand Inquisitor, was a loyal Dominican. At Torquemada's behest, some 8,800 were burned at the stake. Well over 100,000 suffered other penalties.

TWELVE YEARS AFTER Dominic's death, his stone coffin was opened. A sweet fragrance is said to have surged from his exposed bones. It was a scent so delicious, witnesses said, that everyone wanted to get as close as they could, for as long as they could, before the relics were sealed up again in their box. It made them swoon.

More than 100 years later, the bones were exhumed once more. The skull was carefully removed so that it might be placed inside a special golden reliquary of its own. Then the headless skeleton was returned to its white marble tomb.

❖

Well Enough Alone

▼▼▼▼▼

TODAY THE GOLDEN reliquary is mounted behind the tomb. Shaped like a miniature cathedral, it has a window through which stare the empty eyes of Dominic's skull. Attached to a wall nearby is an X ray of the tomb, showing a jumble of bones, taken in the mid-twentieth century. A German tourist points his video camera to the wall. He murmurs "X ray" to rhyme with *fly*.

AT THE FAR end of the church from Dominic's tomb is a deep chapel. Under long shadows, in a glass case against the wall, lies a waxwork so breathtakingly perfect that at first glance the rangy figure inside looks alive, or dead a minute at most. It wears the Dominicans' black and white. Its nose is a great hook, its cheekbones sharp enough to cut butter. Up close, faint veins show blue in the pale waxen brow, and sleek human hair sprouts from the waxen scalp. Casting spiky shadows of their own, its eyelashes are the long dark sort that any girl and many men would envy. Slender, slippered feet protrude from under the black cassock's hem.

No bones are hidden inside this waxwork. The relics of the man in question reside in a honey-colored stone urn on a pedestal across the chapel. The waxwork is merely a doll, though more beautiful if more morbid than most.

Now known as Blessed James of Ulm, the German mercenary who made brilliant stained-glass windows died in 1491. Beatified in 1825, he awaits his sainthood.

At twenty-five, James Griesinger left his home on a pilgrimage to Rome. Like the *Minnow*'s crew on *Gilligan's Island,* he planned just a short visit, but circumstances prevented him from ever going home again.

Inept planning found James in Rome without enough cash for his return journey. He knew he must find work. Though he had been trained throughout his youth in glassmaking, he sought an entirely different career: one that promised drama along with room and board.

As a mercenary in a Neapolitan duke's army, James had no trouble reconciling the arts of war with the faith that had drawn him to Rome in the first place. His only trouble was with his comrades-at-arms. Their behavior shocked and disgusted him, and they made great sport of his vow of chastity.

In despair he fled. Finding work as a servant in a wealthy home, James performed menial tasks for several years until he felt he had accumulated enough money for his journey back to Germany. He set off, but by the time he reached Bologna he was broke again.

Here he joined another local army. As a resident soldier, he regularly attended the church of St. Dominic, whose energetic Dominican preachers he liked. He traded his battle gear for a cassock. Drawing on skills he had learned in his youth, he began fashioning stained-glass windows. His moody emerald greens and sapphire blues created biblical scenes that sprang to life in sunlight.

A PAINTING IN the chapel shows James in black, praying before an airborne Virgin and the baby Jesus. A gigantic nose and rodential overbite are the painter's pointed way of showing us that James would win no beauty contest. But the figure in the painting does not seem to care. His dark eyes raised, his fingers clutch a rosary. They are the long and slender type of hands I have always thought belong to artists alone.

Corpus, reads the plaque over the casket, to inform us that this is a sculpture of a dead man.

The chapel is empty of visitors. But five of the thousand-lira candles on the wrought-iron votive tree before the waxwork have been lit. The tree's curving boughs can be spun every which way independent of each other for a lazy

Susan effect. The red glass shielding the candles makes red blossoms pulse and tremble on the marble floor

SET INTO THE wall on the waxwork's left is a niche. Mounted within, fitting its domed space as if made to do so, is what appears to be the detached head and shoulders of a corpse.

Swathed in a cowl, the taut-skinned head tilts as if listening thoughtfully to music. Taupe like potato peel, the head looks mummified. Its cheeks and chin are gaunt but well-defined, its lips partly ajar, half-smiling with eyes closed as if to say *Oh well, I'm dead.* It must be awkward, though, to cut a body just below the shoulders.

A sign explains this is a work of papier-maché. Then it goes on to declare that the relics of a much-loved theologian are "in this place." But it does not say exactly where the relics are, or what parts they comprise. It does not say whether or not the papier-maché was applied directly to the dead man's flesh, the way in school we laid the sopping strips over inflated balloons.

BACK IN THE crowded part of the church, where postcards are sold, I ask the clerk about this theologian. *Is his head in there?* She does not know, and laughs behind her hand. A monk is summoned. Sunlight falls across his sleeves as the big door opens and shuts. He recites what the sign says, having memorized it. But he'll say no more. Another tour group bustles past us, queueing up at Dominic's white tomb.

"That's what you want to see," the monk says. "Michelangelo."

The Fragrant Grave

▼▼▼▼▼

St. Catherine of Bologna
Corpus Domini
Bologna, Italy

i
IT IS EASY to breeze along a back street past the church called Corpus Domini without even noticing it. Its door is unprepossessing, despite its plaque that heralds this church's connection with St. Catherine of Bologna.

Inside, the church's walls and altar also fail to inspire. Against the silent whiteness of a structure repaired heavily after Allied bombing during World War II, a few old ladies sit in pews and pray.

You might easily enter this church and leave it again without ever noticing a series of small round latticed portholes along one wall on the left. You might not see the buzzer that is set, like a doorbell, into this wall. And you would never ring the bell. Then you would never know.

AT THE SOUND of the bell a door unlocks from within and pops open in the wall. Behind the door is an anteroom cluttered with silvery ex-votos. Beyond this, through another door, is yet another chamber.

It dazzles, golden, a cupola in a fairy tale.

Draperies fall, sky blue with golden tassels, from the round trompe-l'oeil sky of its ceiling. Painted clouds loom overhead in that eternal April. Candelabras shed a white electric glow. Gilt angels, big as leopards, play a silent harp and mandolin. Long golden wings jut from their shoulders, rising far above the angels' curly heads. Long-stemmed white and yellow daisies bob in vases at their feet, and deep pink cosmos, soft as eyelids, presage the cold. Gilt gables ring the chamber, sprouting golden leaves and Grecian geometrics. Trompe-l'oeil bouquets, pink and cream, ascend the walls. Trompe-l'oeil fruit hangs plump from painted vines.

In the middle of all this, a corpse sits up straight in a throne.

POSED UPRIGHT IN a glass-enclosed golden chair, with a big crimson cushion behind, Catherine of Bologna's body sits erect with its head tilted slightly to one side, as if listening. The generous folds of a black and white habit all but hide bare feet as dark as Hostess cupcakes. In its lap, the corpse cradles a book. A gold ring shimmers on its finger. Since her death in 1463, Catherine's face has kept its soft curved contours. But the flesh has turned so dark that from across the room you can discern neither nostrils nor lips.

She wears no satin or brocade as other saints-turned-mummies do, neither a flower garland nor bead-spangled shoes. She was a member of the Poor Clares: nuns whose poverty means much to them. Her dead flesh keeps that vow. And yet the chamber where she stays is nearly blinding.

Still more golden angels cling, in pairs, amid the painted splendor and chiseled conceit of its bright walls. All framed in gold are portraits showing Catherine gorgeous as she paints with a palette while staring heavenward: a young artist, inspired.

THE MAN WHO guards the chapel wears a blue silk suit with a crisp white shirt, and sleek black shoes with buckles. Bologna is a shoe town. He wears thin ribbed socks, nearly a woman's, neatly turned. He sits in one of the four folding chairs facing Catherine's throne. It is his job to sit here all day, the electric light gleaming on his bare head. He prays, kissing his fist, to pass the time.

He hears the buzzer and unlocks the door. A woman rushes in, wearing a high-necked dress whose expensive cut and fine green fabric belies its matronly qualities. A pearl and platinum ring matches her hair.

She kneels on the polished wooden stair behind the barrier that is as close to the throne as visitors can come. Clinging to the railing, she hangs her pale head while mouthing words without making a sound. She rises awkwardly. With a clatter of heels she backs into one of the folding chairs. The guard does not look at her as she flips open a Vuitton bag to extract a rosary whose iridescent beads look well with her ring. She works the beads but makes a snuffling sound. I cannot help but watch. She weeps.

SEEN FROM THE wooden stair, Catherine's lips are sensuous, like Diahann Carroll's. She is matte all over, without the roasted-poultry sheen so typical of mummies. She sits with knees together as if waiting for a train, her posture much better than mine. The carpet leading to the wooden stair is patterned with gigantic roses.

CATHERINE DE' VIGRI'S father, a diplomat, sent her as a girl of ten to a marquis's estate. As an official companion to the marquis's daughter, Princess Margarita, Catherine lived among courtiers, and seemed destined to grow up and marry one of the nobles who inhabited that realm.

The estate was in Ferrara, a city thirty miles northeast of Bologna that was then a great cultural center. So, alongside her friend the princess, Catherine was treated to an education in arts and literature—a luxury virtually unknown among girls of the fifteenth century. Proving herself skilled at composition and calligraphy, she developed a special knack for the delicate art of painting miniatures.

When the princess married she asked Catherine, who was then fourteen, to stay on as always at the estate. But Catherine would not stay. After the wedding she left her wealthy surroundings to join a commune: a group of pious virgins who were waiting to become Poor Clares.

After they took the veil and moved to Bologna, Catherine assumed a nun's typical round of daily chores. To a girl raised in the perfumed shadow of a princess, these tasks must have seemed dull. Yet Catherine forced herself to fit in, vowing to adopt a "perfect" life. She hefted wood, guarded the convent's door and baked its bread.

According to one legend, which recalls a similar one attributed to St. Zita, Catherine had just placed a batch of unbaked loaves in the oven when she heard a bell. It was summoning the nuns to hear a visiting preacher's sermon. If she hurried off to join them, there was no telling what time she might return. Yet she had sworn obedience. Catherine glanced uneasily at the oven as the bell chimed again and she rushed out the door.

The preacher talked and talked. Catherine was horrified as she realized that his sermon had gone on for four hours. She sat trying to focus her attention, but images of charred loaves swirled in her head. As soon as the sermon ended, she dashed back to the kitchen. Flinging wide the oven doors she found the bread a perfect golden brown. Later that day, after their next meal, the nuns remarked that it was the most delicious bread Catherine had ever baked.

ONE FRIDAY NIGHT at the convent, Catherine thought she heard Jesus talking to her from a crucifix.

She was thirty-two when, one Christmas Eve, she sat meditating on the holiday. The Virgin Mary, whose alleged September birthday Catherine shared, played a key role in these imaginings. To show the Virgin she was thinking of her, Catherine decided to recite the "Hail Mary" a thousand times.

She began, and was well into her repetitions when she looked up in surprise to see a vision of Mary herself. Cradling the Christ child in her arms, Mary came closer, as Catherine would later report. Then she lifted the baby for Catherine to hold—an experience that lasted, as Catherine wrote afterward, "a fifth part of the hour."

For many years afterward, the nuns at her Bologna convent would recall those twelve minutes by reciting the prayer a thousand times themselves on Christmas Eve. They used a cord strung with a thousand beads—one for each time.

Catherine experienced other visions as she grew older. Elected abbess, she ran the convent such that it gained widespread acclaim for its austerity. After she died—a few months shy of her fiftieth birthday—Catherine was given a simple funeral as befits a Poor Clare. The nuns carried her corpse to the graveyard without a casket. As they lowered it into an open grave, the nuns were startled at a sweet scent that seemed to issue from the flesh. No flowers or trees grew nearby, nor could anything else account for the fragrance. After earth had been shoveled into the grave and Catherine's corpse buried completely, the scent persisted. As the nuns made their way home, it followed them, wafting across the graveyard and then perfuming the entire district.

A few days later, it was as strong as ever. Some of the nuns returned to the cemetery, ascertaining that the scent was exuding from Catherine's grave.

Less than three weeks after the funeral, pilgrims attracted to Catherine's grave by its persistent fragrance began reporting miracles. Some said their illnesses had been cured by a visit to the grave. It was decided to dig Catherine up.

After lying exposed to the soil for such a long time, the exhumed body was said to have appeared fresh and white, like a brand-new corpse. No sign of decay could be discerned, and witnesses were dazzled at the heady perfume.

AFTER MEDICAL TESTS, and hailed as incorrupt, Catherine's body was placed in a crypt. Months later it was brought back out into the open air, where it was laid prone on a platform for public veneration. After some years, it was decided to seat the corpse upright in a chair, which would afford an even better view. Showing remarkable suppleness, it was duly repositioned.

The long-dead Catherine, herself, appeared in a vision to another nun. Drawing on the artistic skill that had she had nurtured in life, Catherine began dictating her design for a chapel in which she wished her body to be enshrined.

Afterward, all was arranged as she had demanded.

In 1688, more than 200 years after her death, Catherine's

body in its chair was removed from that chapel and installed in yet another, even more lavish.

TODAY, THAT CHAPEL shimmers with all the rococo whimsy of the sort of beauty salon I could never afford. The angels leap with upflung arms. The one playing a mandolin has been festooned with cutout silver hearts dangling from strings: gifts from believers. Daisies blaze against the black of Catherine's dress, reflected in the sheet of glass that was erected to protect these relics after World War II.

ON ONE WALL is a scroll with lines written by Catherine in her lifetime, in Italian:

Who loves the Lord, come to the dance, speaking of love;
Come dancing, all inflamed.

With a heavy sigh, the woman with the Vuitton bag rises to go. Her rosary slides back into the bag with a slippery sound. The watchman in the blue silk suit is careful. In such a small chapel and with so few chairs, he can allow only one pilgrim to enter at a time. Latticed portholes open from the chapel onto the interior of the church. Faces peer in, the buzzer sounds. The watchman would obviously prefer it if I left, as I have been here quite a while, occupying one of the folding chairs and obviously not praying. He lets two women in, and when they leave he lets in two more.

One by one they kneel before the railing, gazing up at Catherine's face, her chocolate hands. The sound of traffic rumbles through the wall. The women bow their heads, their hair reflects the gold. But not for long. They scramble to their feet and hurry through the far door, glancing back, knowing how many other women wait. They are polite.

Ladders to the Sky

▼▼▼▼

ST. ANGELA MERICI
Church of St. Afra
Brescia, Italy

THE NUN'S VOICE ripples through the phone. It is a high, tremulous sound like frying fat. This is one of those calls where you can hold the phone at arm's length and still hear the person's voice. I have told the nun I cannot speak Italian so she has promised to speak French. I do not speak French either, but even so, I know how French sounds and it does not sound like this. The nun's vowels sound all round like Scandinavian, so I am lost.

To see the relics of St. Angela de Merici you have to make an appointment. The convent where they lie, the convent where Angela lived until she died in 1540, is not open to the

167

public. Many residents of Brescia, a sleek and stylish town midway between Milan and Venice, do not know about these relics, although in her own way Angela is perhaps the town's most enduringly famous product.

THE NUN IS saying "eleven" into the phone in every tongue she knows.

And true to her word, she is waiting for me at eleven o'clock. She leads me through a doorway into a big square courtyard open to the sun. Fuzzy-leaved white geraniums overflow round stone pots. Half in shadow, a hose lies coiled under a colonnade. This is the sisters' secret garden. Two feet from the street it flourishes behind a wall, and under lock and key.

Speaking her curious language the nun scoots down the colonnade. She does not look Italian or entirely European and might be Egyptian.

"*Ici*," she says.

She hoists open the door to the Church of St. Afra—a lovely church whose entrance is through the secret garden. Inside, in the white midmorning light, two women wearing cotton shifts and kerchiefs mop the floor. They work doggedly although the floor looks dazzlingly clean already, clean enough to lick. One of the women hauls a bucket, her loose slippers slapping as she moves between the pews. Her suds lurch in the bucket, a sound which the church walls amplify, obligingly.

A SMALL GLASS casket, child-size, rests in a curved chapel to the right of the high altar. Trompe-l'oeil clouds are painted on a bright blue trompe-l'oeil sky overhead, following the local fashion. Trompe-l'oeil leaves climb the walls as if we have not left the garden.

In the case, the mummy's white dress has turned the color

of French vanilla ice cream. The child-size head wears a tiara fashioned out of gold and silver wire, studded with deep blue cut-glass gems. The bony fingers rest atop a pink cushion. One hand thrusting from the satin sleeve holds a bouquet of lilies made from silver filigree: a symbol of virginity. The other holds a walking stick. The body lies below a golden shield resembling motel soap. Engraved across the shield is *Angela M.*

WHEN ANGELA'S ELDER sister died suddenly, she never received the last rites. Still a child, and still reeling from the loss not long before of both her parents, Angela prayed for a sign that would tell her where her sister's soul was.

Sure enough she drifted into an otherworldly state and saw what she was sure was her sister standing beside the Virgin. Angela recognized various saints lingering nearby and decided that she was looking straight into heaven.

After this experience, the child flung herself deeper and deeper into religion. She shunned material possessions and refused to sleep in a bed, preferring the floor. Naturally slim and petite, she trained herself to live on bread and water. Sometimes she ate only once a week.

By the time she was twenty, Angela's intelligence was the talk of the region. She knew Latin, could effortlessly interpret any biblical passage and had a curious gift—St. Anthony is said to have had it too—for memorizing everything she read. Her skills made her a suitable catechism teacher. Her students startled her. Raised mostly on her own, Angela had never had much contact with other young girls. Now as she addressed her classes, Angela's surprise mingled with despair. Girls, she found, were hopelessly ignorant.

For all its wonders, Renaissance Italy held little promise for adolescent girls. Given a choice between arranged marriage or the convent, the great majority grew up without even a minimal education. This robbed women of the right, as Angela saw it, to contribute anything but babies to their own illustrious culture. In society, in art, in science, politics, and all the realms of which history is made, women were virtual nonentities.

Throughout Brescia, Angela gathered a small group of women like herself, most of them self-educated as she was, who agreed with her that the system must be changed. Members of this group took it upon themselves to teach as many girls as they could in the city—holding their lessons in the students' own homes. Granted, they taught more about language and the Scriptures than chemistry.

THE PROGRAM WAS in full swing when Angela had another vision. She saw a procession of girls wearing crowns and dressed in white. They were ascending a ladder made from shafts of light that reached into the sky. A band of angels accompanied their ascent with the sound of their golden harps. Jesus appeared, calling Angela's name.

Not long afterward, she had another vision. This time she saw St. Ursula, who according to popular legend was brutally slaughtered along with eleven thousand virgins on the banks of the Rhine at Cologne. Though she led her companions to their deaths, Ursula is the patron saint of young girls. Angela took the vision as a sign that she had chosen the right path.

Another day, attending mass, she levitated.

Her teaching program was still popular when, in 1524, Angela left Brescia to begin a long pilgrimage. On the Greek island of Crete, only halfway to the Holy Land, she went blind. It was as sudden as it was inexplicable. Staggered by her disability, the aging pilgrim—Angela was now fifty—

insisted on continuing her journey. She toured the Holy Land inhaling its fragrances, tasting its food, and hearing its music, not seeing a thing. Many weeks after leaving Italy, she was on her way home again. The party paused en route in Crete. And there, in the very spot where Angela had lost her sight, she got it back again.

BACK IN BRESCIA, her teaching program was more in demand than ever. The pope asked Angela to bring her expertise to Rome, but she stayed loyal to her native north.

When war broke out in Brescia, Angela fled. Upon her return, crowds rushed out to welcome her. Many were already calling her a saint. Some called her a prophetess.

In 1535, she swore with twenty-eight friends and fellow teachers to devote the rest of her life to educating girls. Though they were not nuns and took no other vows, it was a sisterhood serving God as Angela saw it. She called her group the Ursulines, after St. Ursula. Under her leadership, its members wore ordinary clothes instead of habits. They lived in their own homes, not in a communal convent. This type of arrangement had never been tried before and soon proved irresistible. The Ursulines' membership swiftly doubled, then quadrupled.

Angela washed her own hair just before dying, to save her friends from having to do it afterward. Her corpse was laid out in the church of St. Afra uncovered, for all to see, and so many visitors arrived that the corpse was kept on display for thirty days. In all this time, it is said, the body neither stiffened nor gave off an unpleasant smell. Some said it gave off a *sweet* smell, like perfume.

In 1744, some two hundred years after Angela's death, her corpse was taken from its tomb and examined. It had become a skeleton except for one leg and its head, which

▼▼▼▼▼

was reportedly intact—with one eye open, its iris dark and glistening. Afterward the corpse was dressed in a new set of clothes and set out on display to await eternity behind glass. Long before she was named a saint, people all over Europe were crediting the dead Angela with curing their ills: apoplexy, paralysis, gum disease.

DETERMINED TO LIVE, work, and worship in her own way while leading females out of what seemed a dark closet, Angela was hundreds of years ahead of her time.

Angela's walking stick is pocked, the varnished surface nibbled by woodworms.

The eyes in Angela's brown face are crushed. Under electric bulbs that light the casket from within, the skin gives off a slick but mottled sheen. A framed snapshot on the chapel's wall shows the corpse as it appeared in 1930. A caption explains that in that year, the preservation of Angela's incorrupt relics was enhanced by the application of a natural resin.

The mummy looks worse today than it appears in the picture. Now its lips draw back, baring remarkably large teeth. Time and chemicals have given the saint's face a tautness that could pass for glee.

LIGHT SPLASHES THROUGH the wire mesh on a window that opens onto the garden. Warm wind shirrs the potted ferns arranged around the church. The cleaning women sigh, pushing their mops. The air is heavy with the smell of cleanser.

Sunlight falls across glass chandeliers.

A painting on the altar shows the death of Christ. A dog glowers transfixed, the Virgin grieves. An angel holds a discipline. The wooden Jesus on the crucifix above the altar has short legs, too short, as if the carver became too absorbed making the arms and chest and then ran out of wood.

Angela died when her Ursuline Order was only five years old. Its popularity made it the object of increasing pressure from church fathers, who demanded that the Ursulines buckle down and act like standard sisterhoods. Angela had been dead less than thirty years when St. Carlo Borromeo, a stickler for rules, summoned the Ursulines to Milan and coaxed them to adopt a cloistered, monastic life. Pope Pius V heightened the pressure, imposing strictures that eventually led to the Ursulines' officially taking the veil. As nuns, they lived in convents and operated boarding schools. Ursulines were the New World's first nuns: one chapter settled in Quebec in 1639, another in New Orleans in 1727. But Angela's dream of a company of women, religious yet unfettered, was long vanished.

ALONG THE WALLS and columns in the church of St. Afra, inlaid marble birds perch on furled leaves. They flit past yellow flowers, nibble berries like the ones for sale in town. The cleaning-women rest against their mops chatting about somebody's baby, in this place of death.

Working Stiff

▼▼▼▼

St. Carlo Borromeo
and Blessed Alfred Schuster
The Duomo
Milan, Italy

SHOPPERS CROWD THE streets between the station and the *Duomo*. They walk purposefully, swinging shopping bags bearing designer logos. Two Japanese girls are snapping pictures of each other hoisting Prada bags, posing beside a Vespa which some unwitting Italian has parked beside the potted topiary flanking a *trattoria* called Kisses. In the shop windows along the streets are headless dummies wearing evening gowns and full-length furs in cyclamen and lime.

Which all might make you think Milan is godless.

Then again its cathedral seats forty thousand.

Quieter and darker at least than the street outside, the

Duomo is still somehow no cooler. In its wealth of pews, hundreds of tourists slump cradling their heads, sick with the heat. Sleek marble columns march from one end of the church to the other like a phalanx of gargantuan asparagus. Statuary looms in the darkness near the ceiling. More of it poses all around the worn mosaic floor: among these and larger than life is a flayed man, carved in marble. Erect like a Macy's model, eyeballs thrusting from a mass of veins and sinews, he gazes across the vastness of the church with just a whisper of indignance. This is St. Bartholomew, skinned alive in Armenia. The Duomo is the world's fourth largest church—some say the third. Gianni Versace's funeral was here.

The bronze doors keep opening then swinging shut as white sunlight like knifeblades skims the floor.

From the piazza outside comes the roar of a street-sweeping vehicle, a beehive sound.

IT WAS 1576, during a hot late summer like this one, when Milan sweltered amid the sights and sounds of death. The plague, which had been raging since the previous winter in Venice and Mantua, had finally arrived. The Duomo itself was to blame. Pilgrims arriving from infected towns brought the disease along with all their prayers.

As Milan's epidemic swelled, the governor packed up his entourage and fled the city.

Learning of this, Milan's archbishop refused to leave town. A stern martinet, he was known for a lack of humor that may or may not have sprung from childhood struggles with his chronic stutter. He walked out into the streets and began burying the dead.

THE CHAPEL CONTAINING the relics of St. Carlo Borromeo is down a dogleg set of stairs under the floor of the

Duomo. Just off the church's treasury, it is lit by sconces like a speakeasy, its walls lustrous red. In a recess the massive casket stands, silver on silver. Tiny crystal panes make mullioned windows behind which his body lies.

The corpse is dressed in stately robes. As if to match the casket, Carlo's head is coated in thin silver. True to paintings of the saint, the silversmith made Carlo's nose enormous, like a shark's fin. It's the sort of nose that makes me want to laugh, knowing he will not hear, knowing he missionized and thus earns my dislike. Yet I cannot, caught as I am between sympathy for the dead and fear.

A ticket to the treasury includes this chapel. So a constant stream of visitors files past—tourists who have come to see the Duomo's jewels, they come upon his corpse a little startled. Shuffling down the railing, most of them blink heedlessly. Some cross themselves as if to say *Eh, might as well*. Those from faraway nations toy with Carlo's name. Reading the sign aloud, they singsong, *Boh-roh-meh-oh*. Overhead, enhancing the unlikely sensation that Carlo is entombed in a tavern, electric candles rear crookedly from a chandelier.

The silver coating on his head gives him a Tin Woodsman effect.

Behind the glass he looks somehow insistent, as if unaware that most who visit him don't know and do not care what-all he did.

BORN IN A count's castle overlooking Lake Maggiore, Carlo had a Medici for a mother.

He was twenty-two when a courier from Rome brought Carlo an urgent summons. Carlo's uncle—his mother's brother, the former Cardinal Giovanni de' Medici—had just become the pope.

Working Stiff
▼▼▼▼

When Carlo reached Rome, the newly elected Pius IV announced that he was appointing him chief administrator of all the papal states. In effect, Carlo would be the pope's secretary of state. As if that was not enough for any young man, Pius also named his nephew the official Protector of Portugal, of the Low Countries, of Catholic Switzerland, and the Knights of Malta.

Carlo's list of new jobs was not yet complete.

Pius declared him archbishop of Milan.

But Carlo was not a priest.

HE EMBRACED HIS new challenges with the dogged pragmatism that would mark his entire career. Negotiating regularly with kings and emperors, Carlo juggled a staggering array of tasks. Though clerics in many nations were under his command, he remained unordained. But then his elder brother died unexpectedly in 1562. At twenty-five, Carlo had become overnight the head of his large and courtly family. His parents having died some years before, Carlo was expected to wed promptly and assume control of his sisters' futures. The prospect of marriage drove Carlo into the priesthood once and for all. He had himself ordained.

AS A PRIEST, reform became his passion. Lavish churches must be stripped of their ornaments. Lush-living clerics must be subdued. Carlo scoured abbeys and convents in search of anything that might prove fodder for scandal.

He made enemies.

One night, Carlo was in the middle of evening prayers. A motet was under way, and the music muffled the sound of a door opening and a man walking into the sanctuary. Before anyone in the assembled crowd knew what was happening, the stranger had shot Carlo.

As tumult erupted and Carlo crumpled to the floor, the gunman slipped away into the night. But soon Carlo realized that the bullet had merely penetrated his robes, not his flesh. He picked himself up and, with his characteristic pragmatism, continued his prayers where he had left off.

Within a few days, the assailant was identified as a priest. Father Jerome Farina, who fired the gun while wearing laymen's clothes, had been hired by three other priests. Carlo announced that he had forgiven all four. Milan's judicial system felt differently, and two of the plotters were beheaded. Farina and the fourth priest were hanged.

WHEN A FAMINE seized the region in 1570, Carlo gathered provisions wherever he could and is said to have fed 3,000 starving Milanese every day for three months. Then the plague struck.

Carlo took charge, aiding the sick and disposing of corpses. He had altars constructed in the streets so that the ill and dying could see them through their windows. But Carlo believed the epidemic was no accident. Certain that it was a divine punishment for sin, he resolved to do penance on the city's behalf. Barefoot, with a rope around his neck, he walked the streets, hoping his torn and bleeding feet could sway God's hand.

THE PLAGUE LASTED more than a year. In its aftermath Carlo kept up an austere lifestyle. He slept on a hard board and ate almost nothing.

Late in 1584 he developed an infection in his leg. It spread, and he died feverish in the arms of the Welsh priest who was his confessor. The attendants who prepared Carlo's body for burial carefully removed the hair shirt he wore under his vestments. It had scraped his skin like steel wool, leaving red and raw patches. And the corpse's shoulders were riven with the healed welts that years of flagellation had left behind.

Crowds gathered when they heard Carlo had died. After he was buried, pilgrims began bringing preposterously valuable gifts to his grave. Rings and lumps of gold lay scattered on it. Carlo's canonization in 1610 drew more such gifts than ever before. Devotees left nearly 11,000 silver votives around his relics, and nearly 10,000 pieces of jewelry.

Carlo is anything but endearing. Not a hotdogger in the way of other saints, Carlo could not levitate as Catherine did. He could not heal the sick or raise the dead or be in two places at one time, nor did he have splendid visions in which Jesus gave him an engagement ring.

He was merely a hard worker who spent his adult life doing unpleasant tasks and earning a reputation as a complete wet blanket.

It is no wonder that all but the most pious visitors today file past Carlo's relics almost hurriedly. He was a scolder. This city of glamorous fashion models, of high-powered banks and thousand-dollar handbags smacks of the luxury that Carlo yearned to destroy. His presence puts a sense of unease in the air—as if we suspect that our sins are capable of launching another plague.

BACK UPSTAIRS IN the Duomo, near the statue of the skinned man, is yet another glass-windowed casket containing a corpse. This one's head, like Carlo's, is coated in silver. But this face is pretty, even delicate, its pointed nose straight as a tile. The corpse's white-gloved fingers hold a crozier. Red socks produce a playful look under the corpse's slim black shoes with big square metal buckles.

The body belongs to Alfred Schuster, who was archbishop of Milan some 400 years after Carlo held that office. Alfred's casket, more modernistic and spare than Carlo's, bears on its lid a life-size bronze replica of the costumed corpse within. From far away, it looks like twins asleep in bunkbeds.

AN ITALIAN TOUR guide is shepherding a man with two small children through the Duomo. When they pass Alfred's corpse, the little boy shrieks and buries his face in his father's leg. The guide tries to calm him by explaining that the corpse is holy.

He served as archbishop from 1929 to 1951, she says fondly, though the dates appear to leave the boy unmoved. In 1996, the pope beatified Alfred. So he is no longer an ordinary man but not yet a saint.

"He is at that step in between," the guide croons. The child, perhaps envisioning someone suspended in space, begins to sob.

Alfred is credited with miraculously restoring a blind nun's sight. But the charismatic archbishop earned most of his fame by aiding Italian Jews during World War II. Despite or even because of his own German heritage, he fought the fascists' anti-Semitic laws and begged Mussolini to surrender. He aided his counterpart in Genoa, Archbishop Pietro Boetto, in his efforts to help Jews escape the country to safety, well before the rest of the world grasped the reality of Hitler's death camps.

HIS MOUTH SEALED with silver, Alfred awaits sainthood.

Eating from the Dog's Dish

▼▼▼▼

St. Germaine Cousin
Parish Church
Pibrac, France

PIBRAC IS A stop on the commuter train line from
Toulouse. Beyond the narrow concrete platform with
its self-service ticket machine stands the ruin of its decommissioned station. Broken cinderblock and shattered glass
surround the abandoned building whose entrances, still
marked *Sortie* and *Chef de Gare*, have been sealed with
bricks and mortar. Spray-painted graffiti leaps across the battered walls. It is a script textured like sofa cushions: splats
that might be letters, might be runes.

This is the kind of country town where, like St. Germaine,
generations died where they were born.

Stenciled across the wall, a woman in a swimsuit says in English, in a word balloon, *Come on I want it.*

In the shattered glass behind the platform are spent lighters, gum wrappers, Cacolac bottlecaps. The small-town wind riffles the liquidambar trees across the track. White moths rise from the grass. A girl with a long ponytail paces the platform. About the age at which St. Germaine died, she clutches her suede coat around herself, waiting to depart, and sighs.

ITS BELL TOWER jutting into a blue velvet sky, the parish church stands on a summit in the center of a town that feels deserted on a summer day. Warm winds huff up and down the quiet streets. They toy with the awning on a bakery behind whose window nutted loaves jut from a vase but nothing moves. Beyond the town, the countryside lies low and green, the pastures stirring in the wind and streaked with silver.

Wind buffets the church. Far humbler than Pibrac's basilica across a tree-lined esplanade, this one still holds the trump card. Erected in a style favored by the medieval Knights of Malta and ever so slightly resembling a fort, this church is the one Germaine herself attended every day, leaving her sheep behind. And this is the one that holds the relics of the saint.

A baby's pacifier gleams among the folded notes and snapshots on the pedestal that holds what's left of St. Germaine. No bigger than a steamer trunk, her gleaming bronze-and-glass reliquary is fashioned after a cathedral, with Gothic archways and spires. Yet a statuette of the pious little shepherdess is mounted atop its roof, as if she were a chimney sweep. Through the glass you can see a waxwork. It is neither a perfect replica like James of Ulm's waxwork in Bologna nor a clumsy mannequin like Maria Goretti's in Nettuno. With its too-pretty face, this one has its origins written all over it: France at the dawn of the nineteenth century. Its eyebrows are slim and immaculately arched against a brow smooth as milk. The painted rosette of its lips bespeaks a lovely acquiescence as convincing as a bisque doll's. Meant to resemble Germaine with its hands clasped and its face deathly pale, the figure is far too small for a girl who died at twenty-two. It also lacks the oozing sores and chunky scars that made Germaine's life such hell. Nor does it reproduce the withered hand that so disabled her.

A mustard-colored brocade dress lies heavily over the figure. Sequinned slippers cap its tiny feet.

After it was exhumed by accident and found incorrupt following her death in 1601, Germaine's corpse lay for years in this church for all the world to see. Then, during the French Revolution, Catholic churches and relics fell into popular disfavor. Rioters tore the corpse from its shrine. Doused in quicklime, Germaine's flesh sizzled away. Only the bones remained. Believers picked them up later and cleaned them off. Today the waxwork hides them.

Cobwebs flutter from the reliquary, yet it's not as if this shrine has been neglected. Up against the wall a set of steps is lined with dozens of bouquets. Tall votive candles hiss, exhaling warmth. A guestbook stands open, its pages dark with scribbled messages and curling in the damp. Notes cram the slot between the casket and its pedestal.

The pacifier has been sucked. Its yellow plastic is scuffed, the rubber tip distended. On its ring a cartoon dolphin winks while spouting.

SOON AFTER GERMAINE Cousin was born in 1579, her mother died. She left behind a sick child. Not only was Germaine's wrist twisted so as to render her right hand useless. Scrofula affected her lymph glands, making her neck swell grotesquely. Suppurating sores opened on her right cheek and neck, oozing fluid.

Germaine's father was quick to remarry. But his bride, the new Armande Cousin, was a widow who had already lost three daughters of her own and felt only disgust for the baby who was taking their place. Terrified of contagion, she is said to have made Germaine a pariah in her own home as her husband looked on. Germaine's father—like Cinderella's, in the tale that this saint's so strongly evokes and which also comes from France—was by all accounts gutless.

They say Armande once abandoned Germaine in a sewage ditch for three days. They say she poured boiling water on the little girl's legs. They say she fed Germaine so sparsely at mealtimes that the child crept on the floor to filch her dinners from the dog's dish. In time, Armande and Germaine's father had babies of their own. Determined that her own children must not become infected with Germaine's disease, Armande decided to bar the sick girl from her house. Sleeping in a stable, Germaine ate whatever scraps her stepmother sent out to her. Every day she led her father's sheep to pasture. As old sores healed and new ones broke open, scars studded her cheek and neck.

Illiterate and with no human company, Germaine spent long hours outdoors. Growing more and more devout in her loneliness, she is said to have made a rosary from a knotted string. She knew no prayers by heart but, it is said, she begged God to keep her from starving to death—and she begged him for a way to please Armande.

Watching Germaine's burgeoning piety in all its simple-mindedness, villagers called her "the little bigot."

Every day she left her sheep alone in the fields for a while as she walked back into town and went to church. Although wolves infested the Boucône forest surrounding the fields, it is said that none of Germaine's sheep was ever harmed.

The disabled little shepherdess had to cross the Courbet River on her way to church. Witnesses later said they remembered seeing her walk on water when the river was in flood. Some said they had seen the river part to let her cross.

Life on the farm offered only sorrow. Taking cues from their mother, Germaine's half-siblings would use ashes to taint the scraps of food they brought her in the stable. When her back was turned they smeared tar on her clothes.

Those years of abuse and neglect surely colored her mind, her sense of herself, her way of looking at the world. And although she must have been nearly crazed with cold and hunger, Germaine began deliberately increasing the sufferings her family imposed on her. Cutting her already sparse diet down to bread and water, she took to shunning food altogether, giving her meals to beggars. She became obsessed with the heretics she knew lived in nearby towns and punished herself thinking this would atone for their sins.

Germaine's legend includes an episode that recurs in those of several other female saints—the servile Zita, for example. It is said that on one freezing winter morning, Armande stepped outside to find a beggar sleeping in the stable where Germaine dwelt. At that moment, she saw Germaine hurrying across the farm with something bundled in her apron. Certain that her stepdaughter had stolen food with which to feed the man, Armande accosted her, tearing at the apron. Germaine released her bundle. No food tumbled out onto the icy ground but, instead, handfuls of summer flowers.

Germaine, it is said, picked up a bright blossom by its stem and offered it to the woman who had destroyed her childhood.

THE STUNNED ARMANDE asked Germaine at once to return home and live in the house with the rest of her family.

Germaine refused. One morning not long afterward, her father realized the sheep had not been taken out to pasture. Though Germaine never overslept, he strode out to the stable to wake her. There he found his daughter dead, at twenty-two.

GERMAINE'S DEATH, LIKE her life, caused not a stir. The town of Pibrac hardly cared that a half-daft and ugly young woman had expired on a farm. Buried in the parish church which she had visited so many times, Germaine Cousin was promptly forgotten.

More than forty years later, workmen repairing the parish church accidentally broke open an old unmarked grave. What they reportedly found was not the fleshless skeleton of a woman long dead but a body perfectly preserved. The lush hair on its head was garlanded with carnations and rye.

The workmen summoned others to inspect it, but no one could identify the corpse. At last two elderly people pointed out its withered hand and the scars that told them it must be the body of a girl they dimly remembered: Germaine Cousin.

The corpse was put on display near the church's pulpit. As more and more visitors came to marvel at it, many claimed the dead Germaine was able to heal diseases. A boy with a tumor on his hipbone that is said to have promptly disappeared was among these. A noblewoman believed that her visit to Pibrac's church had cured the cancer in her breasts.

Attention focused on Germaine. Who had this young woman been, and what had she done to merit an incorrupt corpse?

Incorruptitude—a dead body's refusal to putrefy—has always been taken as a sign of sanctity. In Germaine's case as in others, it has led to canonization proceedings. We hear story after story of exhumed corpses looking fresh and plump, even spurting fresh blood when cut.

Pointing to archeological finds in Egypt and Peru among other places, scientists argue that given the proper soil and air conditions, any corpse can mummify naturally. And it is true that the saints' relics displayed in Europe and hailed as incorrupt more often resemble Egyptian mummies, with their taut discolored skin clinging to their bones, than corpses freshly dead. Like much else, it takes much faith to believe in incorruptitude. But thousands do.

While the bodies of celebrities like Catherine of Siena and Anthony were exhumed purposely in hopes of finding incorrupt corpses, Germaine would be unknown today—much less a beloved saint—if it were not for some workmen's errant shovels.

In gratitude for her cancer cure, the noblewoman presented Pibrac with a lead casket in which to keep Germaine's remains. The ensuing years brought many claims of miracles. In 1661 and again in 1700 Toulouse's vicars-general opened the casket, signing depositions attesting to the body's incorrupt condition. Medical tests performed at that time declared that the corpse had never been embalmed.

Pilgrims flocked to the church. They asked the sick girl to make them healthy.

IN 1793 THREE revolutionaries led by a tinsmith named Toulza stormed into the church. Tipping Germaine's body out of its lead casket, they immersed it in quicklime. Then they shoveled soil over the seething mass.

After the revolution had subsided, Germaine's bones were extracted from the soil. The quicklime had done its work.

By 1850, over 400 documents had been assembled to support Germaine's sainthood. The writers claimed Germaine's relics had cured congenital as well as acquired infirmities, including spinal damage and blindness. Thirty French bishops and archbishops wrote letters recommending that the obscure shepherdess be canonized.

TODAY, A SNAPSHOt rests among the many left behind by pilgrims on Germaine's altar in the parish church. It shows a woman seated at a table cluttered with the remnants of a festive meal. Champagne bottles shine amid white plates slick with chunks of fat. The woman's dark hair is bobbed short. She holds aloft a drained champagne glass and smiles tentatively. Her smile reveals a gap between her teeth. Nothing is written on the back—not that Germaine could read, anyway.

Some of the notes left behind on the altar are composed carefully with fine penmanship on cards and flowered stationery. Others are scrawled on pages torn from magazines, on Post-its and receipts, the debris fished out of some woman's purse.

"Let Daniel and Chantal have a good trip."

"Let Papy and Mamy have a happy retreat."

"Banish all that is negative in me, all that is impure, unlucky, evil."

"Give me health and happiness at your discretion."

"Give us the teachings of your sweetness."

"I have many great problems."

Someone has tied a twist of white netting, perhaps a swatch of wedding dress, around one corner of the casket.

SOME DEVOTEES SAY that God chose to render Germaine's body incorrupt in order to teach a lesson that ugly girls are really beautiful inside. If any country needs to learn this lesson, it is France.

Germaine's devotees—and tens of thousands come here every year—beg her for miracles. Yet at the same time they are proprietary. They coddle Germaine, as if to erase the abuse her own family gave her. They treat her shrine with all the care befitting a motherless daughter banished, ill, from her own home. Just as they'd try to cheer a sick girl, pilgrims fill the shrine with gaudy things. The marble steps are packed with flowers. Pink fake roses with their paper petals dipped in glitter, as if no amount of shine could ever be enough. Florists' gladiolus tinted blue, the blue of swimming pools. White plastic lilies. Sweet alyssum, snipped from some back garden, stuffed into a vase shaped like a ballerina. Ferns. A bird of paradise. Live orchids drooping in a paper box that reads *Orient Orchid*.

Oranges and lemons in a basket.

The saint's life story, written on a posterboard with Magic Markers, hangs on a wall. It is a crooked script, half capitals. Its stylized *s* and *e* remind me of how gang girls at my junior high school signed their names. Scrawled flowers decorate the story: tulips shaped like nozzles.

"*Une pauvre . . . une souffrante . . . mal-aimée*," the text reads: Poor girl . . . sufferer . . . unloved.

She is the patron saint of the disabled, and of victims of abuse, and children who have lost a parent.

Votive candles crowd a table in the corner. Many of these are the tall kind, frosted white and imprinted with pictures of a simpering Germaine with her sheep. Some bear souvenir slogans, "*Priez pour nous—PIBRAC*."

The guest book's pages curl up from the damp. I pore over the book, finding that guests have come here from Saigon, London, all over France. "Thank you for giving health," one writes. "Please think of Cécile," writes another, "we've been praying for her."

As I flip through the pages, a woman rushes into the chapel. Her high-heeled patent-leather mules clack on the stone. She wears a yellow raw silk suit. Her hair stands up in peaks, assaulted by the wind. She wears a lot of blush; it makes purplish clouds across her cheeks.

She asks me where to buy a candle in a voice broken and hoarse, like someone scraping bones across a pavement.

"Just there," I say, pointing toward the gift shop, "on the left."

When she comes back she holds two tall votives, one in each hand. She bends over the table lighting them. They flash and gutter, gilding her lap. She stands breathing smoke, the sick girl behind glass between us.

A Murdered Child

▼▼▼▼▼

Brantôme Abbey
Brantôme, France

AN ABBEY MARKS the far edge of the little town. It
presses up against green cliffs like a gigantic slice of cheese-
cake. Carved into the cliffs are caves the monks made in this
soft stone long ago, in which to pray and store their wine,
and raise fish which they ate. The abbey stands between the
hills and Brantôme, with its sparkling river and mecieval
lanes that curve and spur with all the logic of intestines.

Earlier incarnations of the abbey were destroyed first by
the Vandals and then the Visigoths during the fifth century.
Four hundred years later it had been rebuilt when the

Normans shattered it again. Nor would it survive the Hundred Years War.

Brantôme's abbey would rise again. It always did. It housed a precious relic that a constant stream of pilgrims yearned to see: the small bones of a baby.

IN THE ABBEY today, a tape-recorded Gregorian chant is pulsing through speakers mounted on the wall. A young Australian couple, their accents giving them away, are lighting votive candles for the Virgin. Wearing army-surplus trousers, they elbow each other playfully while using one flame to ignite another. In the trembling light the woman's blonde curls drift across her freckled neck like suds.

"Stop hitting me," the man squeals.

The chant falls then rises, with a sound like wrack washing slowly ashore. But when it ends, the cassette crackles into silence for a minute before a New Age melody wafts through the speakers into the church.

The young man's head jerks up from his candles.

"That's an oboe," he hisses.

MOUNTED HIGH ON the wall on the far side of the abbey is a small cathedral made of bronze and glass. It is a reliquary for a child. No bigger than a toaster oven, it has spires and lofty archways. To see through its windows I must stand on tiptoe, on a plastic chair. Behind the windows lies a baby doll.

One porcelain hand rests on its breast. Rich yellow hair surrounds its porcelain face. It makes no effort to pretend that it is anything besides a doll. It smiles.

HAVING BROUGHT WHAT may or may not be St. Thomas' finger back to Rome after her fourth-century pilgrimage, the empress Helen—*St.* Helen—also brought home a great many more of her purchases. Among them were the remains of a baby. With her own hands, the empress herself is said to have dug the remains from a Bethlehem graveyard.

After reaching Europe, the relic changed hands several times. At one point, among other spoils of war, it came into the possession of a Muslim caliph.

The caliph gave it to Charlemagne. This Frankish king and head of the Holy Roman Empire loved relics so much that under his rule during the ninth century every church was *required* to house them. After acquiring the baby's tiny bones, he awarded them with great pomp to the abbey in Brantôme. His gift would transform this riverside village into a thriving hub.

THE BONES WERE said to be those of a boy killed under King Herod's orders when Jesus himself was still a child. The baby was not singled out for murder, but was one of many felled during a bloodbath. No history book in the world records this, though the Book of Matthew tells how it began—and how its victims came to be known as the Holy Innocents.

As the Book of Matthew begins, three wise men arrive in Jerusalem marveling over a star they have seen in the east. Certain that it heralds a newborn king of the Jews, the wise men are on their way "to worship him."

Hearing this news and wanting to learn more, Herod assembles his priests and scribes. They tell him of a prophecy in which a Bethlehem-born baby will grow up to rule Israel.

Bridling at the prospect of such a rival, Herod summons the wise men, variously known as the Magi and the Three Kings. He asks them to send word as soon as they find the child so that Herod, too, can join in the worship. The wise men go on their way. They have been warned in a dream not to trust Herod. After presenting Jesus with lavish gifts when they find him, they sneak back to their own country by an alternate route.

Joseph, too, has been warned in a dream of impending danger. In the middle of the night he flees with Mary and Jesus to Egypt.

Hearing nothing from the wise men and realizing that they have duped him, Herod takes matters into his own hands. Insisting that the would-be king must die, he sends out armed troops. Their mission is to kill every little boy aged two or less in Bethlehem and its surrounding region.

When the slashing is over, every boy is dead indeed. Herod is yet to discover that Jesus, safe in Egypt, has survived.

In all their multitudes, the Holy Innocents are hailed as Christianity's first true martyrs: dying, as they did, some thirty years before Jesus did. Conservative theologians suggest that if the slaughter happened at all, its death toll may have been much exaggerated—that it was closer to twenty than to the huge numbers usually reported.

Helen reached Bethlehem hundreds of years after the slaughter is said to have taken place. She was guided to a graveyard where she extracted one skeleton to represent all the young victims. Yet you have to wonder—since the slaughter happened long before Christ became known—whether anyone would really have bothered to record where the babies were buried. Could this be yet another of the arguably shady deals that have earned Helen her reputation as one of history's greatest suckers?

Helen is unlikely to have found headstones in the graveyard where she unearthed the baby's bones. The baby was subsequently dubbed St. Sicaire. This appears not to have ever been an actual given name in any country. Stemming from the Latin word *sica*, meaning dagger, it alludes to the slaughter instead.

A Murdered Child

▼▼▼▼

Like St. Ursula and her shiploads of murdered virgins, the Holy Innocents were all declared saints and as such assigned a collective feast day. In Britain this was celebrated for centuries as Childermas every December 28. As a traditional part of the day's observance, parents are said to have beaten their children lightly while the youngsters lay in their beds.

IN *THE GOLDEN BOUGH*, Sir James Frazer writes of a custom still current in southwestern France as recently as the 1920s. Peasants bent on revenge, he writes, would sometimes cajole corrupt priests to perform a rite called the "Mass of St. Sécaire." Few clergy knew the mass at all, and "none but wicked priests" would dream of doing it.

In a ruined or abandoned church in the dark of night, the priest arrives—with his lover—to mutter the regular mass backwards. He begins precisely at eleven o'clock and finishes at the stroke of midnight. To ritually destroy some enemy of whomever hired him, the priest blesses a black wafer and consecrates not wine, Frazer explains, but water from a well in which the corpse of an unbaptized infant has been placed. He makes the sign of the cross on the floor with his foot and performs other strange gestures. The unwitting victim withers gradually from that night forward, never knowing that the Mass of St. Sécaire is what will kill him.

It is anyone's guess how the dead baby's name became attached to what could pass for black magic.

MEDIEVAL PILGRIMAGE ROUTES included a stop at Brantôme's abbey. On the day I visit, nearly 1,000 years after its heyday, no one is in the church at all except the two Australians, and after their laughter snuffs out a candle they go. Sicaire's reliquary, his bones allegedly obscured beneath the baby doll, hangs ignored on the wall. Why a child's relics should be mounted too high for even an adult, much less another child, to see is a mystery. Perhaps it is to discourage thieves. Anyway the reliquary is dwarfed by a hulking white marble statue that rears, larger than life, from its mountain of a pedestal.

It captures a murder about to happen.

Swinging his arm high over his head, a nearly naked man with Mick Jagger's lips stands with his legs wide apart. A headband crowns his flowing hair. At his feet a young woman flails, cradling her child with one arm while barring the man's way with the other. A veil streams down over her shoulders, past breasts mostly bare. She looks about to scream.

The assailant shall overpower her. In his upraised fist is a dagger as long as his arm. He pushes the woman away to take aim at the child, who frets in its mother's grasp. Just a glimmer of awareness dawns in its wide-open eyes. INNOCENTI is chiseled into the pedestal. The statue is dated 1900 and, thinking to distract us with the dagger, its sculptor exposes great tense expanses of thigh.

AT THE FAR end of the church, above the high altar, Sicaire's murder is depicted all over again, this time in a stained-glass window. It does not mirror the statue. On the window, the killer wears a toga and Roman sandals. Sicaire's mother is nowhere to be seen as the child dangles helplessly by one arm from the killer's hand. The hand looks almost gentle. Yet the Roman's eyes are mean, his weapon drawn. The child stares straight at you resignedly, a golden aureole around his head.

Glass panels read *Ora pro nobis S. Sicarius.*

Pray for us.

Which makes you wonder whether babies pray, dead babies anyway. It makes you wonder whether it is nice to ask a murdered child to pray for us. It seems a burden, too great a responsibility, just as we would never ask an infant to take our suits to the cleaner's.

Yet the presumption is that as a saint, even a very tiny saint, Sicaire must bite the bullet. He must tackle all the tasks expected of his grown-up colleagues. Like the patriarchal Paul, the scholar Augustine or any number of bishops this baby must answer our call, must intercede on our behalf with heaven's top dogs. Even if he'd rather just drink milk.

Beside the statue is a single china vase. Packed with mums and sprigs of pine the vase is hand-thrown and dense, glazed blue and white. Someone has fixed its broken lip with yellow glue, making a gift for a baby.

Love Hurts

▼▼▼▼▼

ST. MARGUERITE MARIE ALACOQUE AND CLAUDE LA COLOMBIÈRE
Visitation Monastery and Colombière Chapel
Paray-le-Monial, France

IT IS THE kind of stormy late-summer day in the French countryside when clouds race, driven, down the sunny sky. Houses and alleys darken as if bruised. From far away you see the rain, in slanting bands that tear the bottoms from the clouds. Along the boulevard the trees mutter and heave.

A Sunday in Paray-le-Monial, a pilgrims' town second in France only to Lourdes, finds all the cafés closed except a Tunisian one. Far to the south, Lourdes trumpets its own fame with gift shops hawking holy-water mints and Mary nite-lites, and with cheek-by-jowl hotels and huge processions. By contrast Paray-le-Monial looks just like any small

Love Hurts

▼▼▼▼▼

Burgundy town, though maybe duller. On a Sunday the streets are empty, and my hotel—one of but a few—is nearly deserted. An illuminated strip affixed to the carpet and running the length of the corridor, as in a theater, gives off a melancholy glow in the silence of the afternoon.

In the tourist office, two clerks sit watching the clouds from behind a counter stacked sparsely with maps of the town. In the winter of 1673, a nun here named Marguerite Marie Alacoque believed she saw Christ tearing out his heart. It was on fire—with love for her. And then he split her chest and took *her* heart and pushed it through the wound in his own chest. She watched it burning, through the hole, before Christ plucked it out again and gave it back to her, pressing it into place.

The other nuns, when they found out, disliked her even more than they already had, which was a lot.

TODAY A SERVICE is in session at the church that houses what is left of Marguerite Marie. This Visitation Monastery is at the moment seeing the afternoon's sole spark of life. Songs rise up from the figures seated in the pews and resound on the soft medieval stonework of the ceiling. Women's voices far outnumber men's, and half the women here are nuns. They sit a little languidly, as if this is their home: the pews their divans and the music so familiar that they hardly have to think. The songs roll off their tongues. Her fingers clasped, one old nun wearing glasses sleeps. She jerks awake every third breath or so, blinking her large gray eyes, to sing a phrase before her head sinks down again.

Above the altar is a Christ whose modern sharpness contrasts with the church, the town, the nuns. Pitched at an angle, he looms sideways as his pierced insteps shoot rays of light. Below him, Marguerite Marie waits on her knees looking at once subservient and priggish.

✣

TO THE RIGHT of the altar, against the wall, lie the relics. A waxwork encases Marguerite Marie's bones. Dressed in the same black Visitation habit as the nuns who sit singing all around it, the figure has the heft and tint of a grown woman barely dead. Its artist would not grant the saint the kindness that was given to Germaine Cousin, whose waxwork in Pibrac displays a beauty Germaine never knew. Such is a gutless kindness anyway. As if to remind us that Marguerite Marie was much despised, the waxwork does not prettify her face. A ski-jump nose and rounded chin which sinks into the fabric of her habit will not endear anyone. A slack-jawed look suggests astonishment at best, though in some lights just as easily suggests stupidity.

A plaque reads, in French, *Awaiting the Resurrection, here lie the bones of St. Marguerite Marie Alacoque.* Drinking glasses on either side are jammed full of carnations, white and pink and striped, like Kleenex daubed with blood. The blossoms nod as if to match the music ringing through the stone.

AT THE AGE of seven—some say as young as four— Marguerite Marie took a vow of chastity out loud. The words simply sprang to her lips. It would be years before she knew what chastity meant.

She so fervently loved going to church that her family grew worried. She upset them further by barraging her body with an array of painful self-punishments. This proved too much for her young flesh, and Marguerite Marie fell ill. Other saints, including Gemma Galgani and Catherine de' Ricci, also suffered extended illnesses that may have been sparked by their severe penances. Scarcely able to move and skeletally slim, Marguerite Marie remained bedridden for four years.

She recovered just in time to begin attending the parties and dances through which young women of her age first tasted society. Soon she came to regret her childish vow. She told herself that holy virginity was not her only option and that if she married, she could still remain as pious as ever by way of penances and charity.

Coming home from a party one night, Marguerite Marie looked up to see Jesus himself. He was standing in her room nearly naked. Blood streamed from the whiplashes crisscrossing his bare back. How could she be so unfaithful, he demanded, when he loved her so obviously, and so much.

Soon afterward, she entered the convent.

Her first assignment was in the nuns' infirmary. There she assisted a sister who soon became impatient with Marguerite Marie's lumbering manner. Aloof and unsmiling, Marguerite Marie blamed the devil for mistakes that she made. She said it was he who always whisked chairs out of reach just as she was trying to sit down in them.

She took up her old regimen of self-punishments again, some of which repulsed the nuns. Rumors spread that she ate patients' excretions in the infirmary.

Like many who have trained themselves to go without food, Marguerite Marie took to daydreaming—often about the region's rich, wine-soaked cuisine. Yet at mealtimes in the refectory she recoiled at the sights and smells. The other nuns avoided her. Too much austerity, they felt, was just another kind of self-indulgence.

KNEELING BEFORE THE assembled nuns one day, Marguerite Marie announced that God had chosen her to be a "sacrificial victim," born to suffer for their sins.

She was twenty-six when one cold day in 1673 a strange sensation came over her. She was sure Christ was paying her another visit. As she later wrote in her autobiography, "I felt myself completely penetrated."

She heard him coaxing her to lay her head upon his breast. She did so, feeling the damp heat of his flesh. Then "he disclosed to me the marvels of his love."

With deft fingers he made a slit in his chest. Marguerite Marie stared as he held apart the corners of his wound to bare his swollen heart. It spouted flame, which Jesus told her was the fire of "love for men, and for you in particular." The organ was full to bursting, he said.

She must make sinners aware of his overflowing love, he told Marguerite Marie. As she later recalled, Christ called her his specially chosen "abyss of unworthiness and ignorance for the accomplishment of this plan."

Still displaying his heart, he asked for hers. Without hesitation she tore open her flesh, reached in and seized it. Handing it to Jesus, she watched as he pushed it through the hole in his chest where it burned along with his own. Moments later he reached in to retrieve it, and Marguerite Marie watched as he held the heart-shaped ball of fire between his hands, placing it himself in the hole between her breasts.

"I give you a precious token of my love," he said.

He went on to predict that this experience would "consume you to the last moment of your life." Sealing the wound on her chest he explained that its pain would last forever.

"You will be able to find relief," he told the dazzled young nun, "only by bleeding."

FOR DAYS SHE went around in a daze, hardly able to speak. She lay awake at night, savoring the sharp pain between her breasts. She did not tell the other nuns about the episode, keeping it to herself. On the first Friday of the following month, she saw Jesus again. The pain in her chest nearly felled her as flames shot from Christ's heart across the room to hers.

The first Friday of the following month she saw him again, and the month after that.

She would later write of encounters in which "I thought I should be consumed . . . and begged him to have pity." She wrote of being "penetrated" as Christ "made known to me the unspeakable marvels of his love."

One day, "my sweet master showed himself to me, resplendant, his five wounds shining like suns. Flames leaped from every part of his sacred humanity, especially from his adorable breast."

She must prove her love, he said, by taking communion as often as possible. She must also make a habit of lying down on the floor at 11:00 PM to "stay prostrate with me for an hour." This would, he said, ease some of his misery.

On the floor, he told her, "you shall do what I teach you."

WHEN ALL OF this was too much for her to contain, Marguerite Marie took the matter to her mother superior. The older nun balked. Among other things, Marguerite Marie insisted that her "master" had "urged me to ask for humiliation." He had also, she said, directed her to tell sinners how much pain their ingratitude caused Christ. She must show them how to honor his heart as she saw it, flaming.

When her mother superior proved unsympathetic, Marguerite Marie took her story to Claude la Colombière, the convent's Jesuit priest. He believed her.

SHE TOLD HIM about all that she had seen. Not only did he hear about her encounters with Jesus, but also about the time when the Holy Trinity paid Marguerite Marie a visit, in the form of three young men dressed all in white. Claude took notes on everything she said.

As a new mother superior was elected who took Marguerite Marie under her wing, the tide began to turn. Claude's writings were made public. The sensation they raised turned Marguerite Marie into a celebrity. In 1688, fifteen years after her first vision of what would become known as the Sacred Heart, a chapel was built in its honor. Marguerite Marie died soon after.

All of Paray-le-Monial lined up for a chance to touch her corpse. Eager mourners snipped away bits of her habit to save as relics.

When the French Revolution broke out, the nuns were terrified that rioters would raid Marguerite Marie's tomb and destroy her corpse as they had so many others. Along with those of Claude la Colombière, her remains were taken from the monastery and hidden in first one private home nearby, then another. In 1817, when the local *curé* died, both relics were in his house. Soon they went back to their shrines.

Believers claiming that Marguerite Marie had cured them of stomach cancer, heart disease, and tuberculosis hastened her beatification. In 1864, as part of the process, clergy gathered one evening by candlelight to prise open her wooden coffin and reveal the corpse. It was a skeleton—except that its head was intact. Some of the assembled clergy hurried to kiss the cheeks and forehead which they later described as smooth and soft. They performed their examination at night, and in private, out of fear that if they did otherwise the crowds would fall on the corpse and dismember it.

IN THE GIFT shop adjoining the church that houses the relics, postcards are for sale showing photographs of Marguerite Marie's disembodied heart. Removed from the bulk of her relics, it has been mounted in a metal reliquary. Behind a heart-shaped crystal pane, the organ is faintly yellow, as if molded of puréed turnip and allowed to dry. The crystal pane is framed by golden flowers, and surmounts a pair of golden angels who resemble young men wearing women's nighties.

"You cannot see it," says the nun behind the counter when she sees how much I like the picture. She shakes her head, eyes downcast. The heart is kept inside the cloister, where only the sisters can enjoy it.

All around the shop, scenes from Marguerite Marie's alleged visions recur over and over on cards, plaques, books, and votive candles. Stained-glass cups depict red hearts aflame and dripping blood, captioned with just one word: *Amour*.

Over and over we see Marguerite Marie on her knees, arms outstretched toward a lover no one else can see. The supplication in her body and her eyes is still, somehow, imperious: as if she knows he comes for her and no one else, that *he* needs *her* and she will not forget this.

Her visions seethe, evoking images from horror films and porn and Harlequin romances. Who could miss the tint of sadomasochism? Flaming organs thrusting in and out of orifices: self-inflicted wounds, at that. Blood flows. Christ thrills the virgin with his promises of how much it will ache. He calls her worthless, ignorant, an abyss, tells her to humiliate herself. She swoons. She lies awake at night delighting in her pain.

Marguerite Marie began stoking her desire for pain while still a child. Many other saints shared this predilection, and it made them famous: Rose of Lima, the New World's first saint, pierced herself with thorns and staggered under the weight of a heavy wooden cross. In some lights the whole idea of penitence, of punishing oneself or being punished, smacks of masochism. So too do protracted martyrdoms. In the name of sanctity we are given vivid blow-by-blow accounts in which St. Cecilia's tormentors, for example, tried to suffocate her in a bathroom. When this failed they attacked her, and before finally dying she lingered for three days with her head partly severed. The attention lavished on details of slashings and dismemberment, of being grilled alive like St. Lawrence or crucified like St. Andrew can only arouse anyone with a penchant for pain.

As you might expect of a young woman in her twenties who joined a convent after being sorely tempted to marry, Marguerite Marie struggled. Shunning food, she wrestled visibly with one kind of hunger. Other kinds taunted her with a dazzling persistence. Her dream lover was the sort whom she could call "my master," and who called her his beloved and his slave.

WHILE THE VISITATION Monastery housing her relics is filled with song that seeps out through its door into the cloudy afternoon, not a soul is in the narrow sanctuary up the street. There, amid modern mosaics shot through with gold and copper tiles, Claude la Colombière's bones lie bound with red string, in a glass-paned box.

Claude's chapel has the grace of having been designed in 1929. It bears a streamlined chic somewhere between the tastes of P. G. Wodehouse's Bertie Wooster and Bauhaus. So its sharp mosaics are a far cry from the bloated angels whom I left behind in Italy.

In broken light the tile glints fitfully. Long shadows race across the floor.

A mosaic shows Francis Xavier, whip-thin. That he is in Asia is apparent from a row of palm trees jutting spikily into a multicolored sky. Kimono-clad Japanese await baptism.

Francis holds a parasol and pours water over the head of a man with slanted eyes and almost feline cheekbones. A lean Angloid angel looks quizzical.

The altar underneath the mosaic is cherry-blossom-pink marble. Standing atop it in all the emptiness and silence is a copper art deco crucifix.

Elsewhere, another mosaic features kneeling harts. Their antlered heads suggest your choice of pagan gods: kachinas or Cernunnos. Christ is in this picture too, enthroned. His chest torn open and his heart exposed, he wears a blood-red robe. The heart simmers amid an opalescent swirl of viscera—the glassy tiles are pearly. Marguerite Marie is there, kneeling as always, along with the Virgin Mary and Claude Colombière. A crowd of nuns is pictured, gaping fawningly, though one of them looks sly.

Flames made of orange tiles leap from Christ's throne into a blue-green sky studded with golden stars. He sits there patiently, his chair on fire.

SWEPT UP IN the gory heat of Marguerite Marie's narratives, Claude championed her cause. She believed Jesus had chosen her to tell the world about his burning heart, and Claude resolved to help her. The blood-specked images and fevered messages that sprang from her lips made their way into his writings, and from there into a world for whom the now-ubiquitous phrase "Sacred Heart" was a brand-new novelty.

After nearly two years in Paray-le-Monial, however, Claude was reassigned to London. There he served as official chaplain to the Duchess of York, whose husband would become King James II. Catholicism was highly unpopular in England. Jesuits in particular were blamed for several attempts on Queen Elizabeth I's life, as well as for King William of Orange's murder in nearby Holland. In 1673,

Britain's Test Act was imposed requiring public officials to swear they did not believe Jesus was actually in the communion wafer.

Claude would not take the vow.

Not long after, a young man posing as a convert gained Claude's trust and then accused him of treason. The priest was arrested.

Held in a dungeon for three years, he lay ill, coughing up blood. France's King Louis XIV intervened to save Claude from the executioner, arranging instead to have the priest exiled and sent home to France. There he died at forty-one. John Paul II sainted him in 1992.

RAISED ON A pedestal, the case holding his bones is adorned with brass block letters spelling *Haec sunt ossa sancti Claude la Colombière*: Here are the bones of Claude la Colombière.

Behind the glass at eye level, Claude's toothless skull could pass for a large and artful caramel. The other bones have been arranged around it on a scarlet velvet cushion trimmed in scarlet cord. Also red is the twine that lashes the bones together. As if to keep any one of them from jumping up and running off, the twine loops around femurs and ulnas, then in and out through the skull's eye sockets, nostrils and between its jaws to effect a complicated knot.

Art-deco mosaics on the walls behind the case depict a rose, a tower, and a rainbow. Fingerprints smear the glass over the bones thickly, as if pilgrims had a habit of rushing to this chapel while eating brioches with their hands.

A bronze statuette of Claude completes a picture that his bones only begin. It shows his horsey face, its fleshy lips. A snapshot posted in the shrine shows John Paul's visit.

Love Hurts

▼▼▼▼▼

IN THE TUNISIAN café, a young couple behind the counter is making kebabs. North African curios hang on the wall: a metal pitcher and a woven shawl that shudders in the wind. The couple's sleek heads bounce in rhythm with the radio. The Smashing Pumpkins shout hoarse promises across the countryside.

The young man slices onions as the song fades out. A new one starts, a driving disco beat, a woman singing English lyrics in a voice as shimmeringly hard as steel.

I'm horny,
I'm hornyhornyhorny.
I'm horny,
I'm horny tonight.

The song pounds through the restaurant, staccato, while the couple sings along. They have the slurred accents of those who know lyrics by heart but don't know what they mean. The girl's black hair swings, fastened with yellow plastic clips shaped like ducklings.

I'm horny, I'm horny tonight.

Her eyes meet mine. Onions and peppers pile up as the grill breathes smoke. The cooks stammer to keep up with the music. They are proud to know an English song.

Blue Eyes

▼▼▼▼

ST. CATHERINE LABOURÉ
Chapel of Our Lady of the Miraculous Medal
Paris, France

IN THE MÉTRO corridor where I enter the system at Odéon a woman is kneeling on the floor playing a koto. The cry of its strings rings out against the tiles. A drunk Frenchman is heckling the musician, shouting *Japon! Japon!* as if the name of her home country is a clever taunt.

In the Métro corridor at Rue du Bac, where I am exiting on my way to see St. Catherine's relics, a Gypsy woman sings. A cross between Gregorian chant and a Hebrew prayer, her song is distended and strange. She clutches a child who wears a shabby woolen hat with fraying kitten-ears on top. She sings one line in a voice that surges like the prow of a boat, pointed and keen, slicing still water. Then she stops. Hanging her head she breathes as if the song is finished. You could have a conversation in between the lines. She starts again, one line, then trails away. As if each line exhausts her or as if she forgets she is singing at all.

THE CHAPEL OF Our Lady of the Miraculous Medal, where the relics are, is not exactly Notre Dame. It is not an architectural nor an artistic wonder, nor is it old as Paris goes. Inside, its decor suggests motel pools and eye shadow and Advent calendars, with swirling pale mosaicked skies and big Ritz cracker haloes. Two grottoes are neo-Byzantine, their red-haired angels lean, with legs straight out of Paris *Vogue*.

Those who find this church are only those who know where to look, as the chapel does not open onto the street. Still, lots of people do know where to look. The crowds who fill its pews prefer to linger here for hours on end. When they go finally, they leave behind their scribbled prayers on slips of paper. Tourists come, but it is Parisians who cherish this church as their own.

The Virgin Mary herself is said to have visited this pastel chapel on an ordinary street. Of all the churches and all the rooftops and all the bridges in Paris, she chose this—if we are to believe the 19th-century nun who claimed it was she whom Mary came to visit.

FLANKED BY MARKETS selling flans and bottled confits and a special kind of giant prune, an unprepossessing gate opens onto the chapel's foreyard. To one side of the yard is a wall whose bas-reliefs illustrate miracles ascribed to the Virgin of the Miraculous Medal. She is called this because, during her alleged visits in 1830, Mary is said to have asked

Sister Catherine Labouré to launch the manufacture of tiny metal ovals in a certain design.

In one of the bas-reliefs, a Jew named Alphonse Ratisbonne is wearing a Miraculous Medal when he sees an apparition of the Virgin and instantly converts. A caption narrates the action. Another bas-relief shows the medal curing seven-year-old Jean Rebit of a terrible ailment in 1932. In yet another, a fire breaks out on the very street where we now stand, rue du Bac, in 1915: Mary appears, looming high over the burning buildings of the Bon Marché. Through her intercession, the chapel emerges unscathed.

On the opposite side of the foreyard is a gift shop selling nothing but Miraculous Medals. Knotted plastic bags, each one bulging with hundreds of medals, line the counter. Hundreds more of them glimmer in racks on the wall, scarcely larger than thumbnails. All are identical. On one side, the Virgin is depicted spreading her arms, surrounded by the words: O *Mary, conceived without sin, have mercy on us who have recourse to thee.* On the reverse, a ring of stars surrounds an M, a cross, a bar, and two hearts dripping blood, one bound with thorns, the other run through with a sword.

AT THE DOOR to the chapel, a sign indicates that one of two galleries is reserved for sick pilgrims. Another is set apart for nuns confined to wheelchairs. An old nun wearing the blue-and-white Sisters of Charity habit is standing outside the door, shepherding the steady stream of visitors. She scolds a man who has a camera, frowning at him until he zips it back into its case.

"It's a house of worship," cries the nun.

Beyond the door, the chapel is packed. A group of pilgrims from Manila all wear matching armbands. Elderly Frenchwomen with their silver hair coiled into chignons hug their coats around them. Brooches glint on their lapels. Here and there, pilgrims are crying softly, stricken at finding themselves in the same place Mary was—not once, but twice. The sound of sniffling echoes through the room, of noses being blown.

OVER THE ALTAR is a large fierce all-white Virgin mounted on a globe, stamping a snake to death. Her crown is bigger than her head. A ring of bright electric lights surround the crown.

Above it all, depicted on the wall in shades of blue and white is Mary seated on a velvet chair and Catherine, kneeling, with her hands in Mary's lap. Angels with cracker haloes hold lilies and watch.

A woman rushes in wearing a matching camel raincoat and beret. The man limping behind her holds a tiny Chanel bag no bigger than a slice of toast.

Catherine's corpse lies near the altar in a glass casket. The flesh looks curiously fresh for having been dead since 1876. The corpse's eyes are open: Catherine's famous blue eyes. In another glass casket across the room, the relics of St. Louise de Marillac are admittedly waxed, and very pretty.

It's a relic bonanza. Mounted on a pedestal and framed in gold is St. Vincent de Paul's disembodied heart.

CATHERINE LABOURÉ WAS ten, and still named Zoë, when her mother died after the last of seventeen pregnancies. Grief-stricken, the little girl declared that the Virgin Mary would now become her new, everlasting mother. As the elder of only two girls living on the family farm in Burgundy, Zoë was expected to shoulder her mother's household tasks—feeding and cleaning up after Mr. Labouré and his many sons. Her younger sister would later recall that Zoë's favorite among her myriad chores was feeding the family's pigeons. She stood shielding her eyes in delight while the hungry birds lunged at her face and tore at her hair.

It was not a schedule that allowed time for school, much less play. Neither able to read nor write, Zoë was not one for speaking either. Passing her days in near silence, she devoted what spare moments her chores permitted to a statuette of the Virgin that she kept in her bedroom.

One night she had a dream she never forgot. She saw herself entering the village church. An old priest whom she did not recognize was celebrating mass. He gazed up at her and beckoned. Zoë was terrified at the sight of this bearded stranger and fled.

SHE BECAME KNOWN in the village as a taciturn young woman, remembered later as unbeautiful except for her blue eyes. When a local boy asked to marry her, Zoë refused. She wanted to be a nun. All she needed was her father's permission and a small trousseau.

Zoë's father would not provide them. Perhaps he wanted her, at twenty, to enjoy a normal married life. Perhaps he hoped she would care for him when he was too old to farm. Believing a stay in Paris would melt her resolve, Pierre Labouré sent his dismayed daughter to visit her elder brother who ran a restaurant in the city.

She had never before left the fields and vineyards of the Cote d'Or, and now she hated what she saw of Paris.

Her brother's wife managed a school for rich girls in nearby Chatillon. There amid brilliantly dressed students much younger than she, Zoë attended the first lessons of her life. But she could not make up for lost time.

One day while visiting a Chatillon convent, she looked up to see the portrait of an old priest hanging on the wall.

It was the priest from her dream.

When Zoë learned that it was Paris's own St. Vincent de Paul, who had died in 1660, she became desperate. She *must* take the veil.

Sidestepping Zoë's father, her brother and sister-in-law got her into the convent. She entered just as the city of Paris was about to hold a huge celebration.

During the French Revolution, which had ended some twenty-five years before, religion was highly unpopular— especially those aspects that, like relics, carried a tint of magic and superstition. Rioters raided churches, dismantling shrines and smashing reliquaries, burning relics or crushing them to bits. St. Germaine Cousin's remains, near Toulouse, were among the casualties. So were those of St. Genevieve, who is said to have kept Attila the Hun from attacking Paris. Her relics, credited with warding off an ergot-poisoning epidemic in 1129, were burned in a Paris square at the height of the revolution.

Amid the unrest, Vincent de Paul's corpse was spirited away into hiding. A few organs and small bits of his flesh had long ago been broken off to be displayed in various shrines, including the convent that Zoë would join, which had an arm bone. But his corpse spent the war years in one hiding place after another, including a private home. By the spring of 1830, Paris felt safe enough that the corpse's guardians decided to bring it out of hiding and put it back where everyone could see it.

Vincent's relics were to be installed in a church around the corner from Zoë's convent. The ceremony surrounding the body's translation from Notre Dame Cathedral, where it was being prepared for display, to its permanent home across the city would go on for days. By now Zoë had taken a new name, Catherine, and she attended the festivities among lavish decorations, music, parades and crowds such as she had never seen.

One evening after walking back to the convent from the celebration around the corner, Catherine lingered beside the reliquary holding Vincent's arm bone. She was startled to see, materializing in midair, a disembodied human heart. It floated before her eyes. Catherine was sure it was Vincent's.

The next evening, returning after a day of festivities, she stopped again before the arm bone. And again as she stood there she saw a gory heart hovering in the air.

The next night she saw it again. Gazing at its slick red surface, she felt a sudden presentiment of disaster.

On the heels of the Revolution, France's monarchy had been restored. Charles X had ascended to the throne in 1824. He was an old man, fiercely conservative, filled with yearning for the *ancien regime*. While the revolutionaries despised religion, Charles was on the Church's side. One of his mottoes was "For Altar and Throne." He envisioned a future in which Catholicism would regain its lost prestige in France—a France whose people bowed low once again to their rulers.

As a nun, Catherine naturally favored the king. The Church's very future was entwined with his. Yet she was no political scientist. Staring across the silence of the chapel at the heart she saw suspended in midair, she felt certain that it presaged Charles's fall.

She was no more of a talker now than she had been as a child. Telling the other nuns nothing of her experiences, she chose as her sole confidant the priest to whom she made confession.

Father Aladel listened for a while, then told her to forget all about what she had seen.

Catherine went on her way. She started seeing Jesus in communion wafers. It went on for months. This time she didn't tell the priest.

Blue Eyes

▼▼▼▼▼

ONE JULY DAY in 1830, the same year Catherine entered the convent, each of the nuns was given an infinitesimal scrap of fabric. Cut from a garment once worn by Vincent de Paul, these souvenirs were "second-class" relics—i.e., items touched or handled by a saint, as opposed to first-class relics which comprised the saints' bodies themselves and third-class relics which were items that had in turn touched second-class relics.

Catherine carefully tore her scrap in half with her teeth, and swallowed one portion.

That night she wakened abruptly at the sound of her name. Catherine jerked up in bed to see a child, its flesh luminous, standing in the middle of her room.

She took it for an angel. Urging her to dress, the visitor told Catherine that someone was waiting for her in the chapel.

Pulling her clothes on, she stumbled down the dark corridor after the luminous child. They reached the chapel together and Catherine, to her surprise, found its door unlocked and its candles alight even though it was past midnight and the entire convent was asleep.

Hearing the rustle of what sounded like silk, Catherine looked up to see a woman wearing a band around her long hair, and a dress whose dreamy white reminded her of the sky at dawn. The woman drew near, sinking into a blue velvet chair near the altar.

Catherine would recognize her anywhere. It was the Virgin.

SHE FLUNG HERSELF onto the floor, her hands in Mary's lap.

The Virgin spoke of disaster.

Charles, she said, would lose his throne. Churches would once again be sacked. Their priests would flee.

"These are," the Virgin said, "such evil times."

When the angel led Catherine back to her room, she saw from the clock that she had been away two hours.

ONE WEEK LATER, Paris erupted in what is now known as the 1830 Revolution.

After a member of Charles's cabinet abolished freedom of the press, printers and publishers all over the city rebelled. Thousands marched in the streets. Soon shopkeepers and others joined the demonstrations. When a few Parisian newspapers defied the law and issued special editions, government forces descended on them. Protests turned into bloody street fights. It went on for three days—which the rebels would call *Les Trois Glorieuses*. Casualties piled up. Charles slipped away and went into hiding.

By the time a provisional government took over, Parisian churches had lost what fragile foothold they had regained under Charles. Catherine could only marvel that the Virgin had been right. In those three days, churches *were* sacked. And bishops were among the imprisoned and the dead.

She had told only Father Aladel about Mary's visit. As before, he bridled, urging Catherine to put it out of her mind. In the months following the summer's skirmishes, as relative peace resumed throughout Paris, he alone knew that a certain young nun claimed to have been vouchsafed a heavenly warning. And he himself had watched it come true.

IT WAS LATE November when Catherine sat in church one evening during a service. Other nuns sat all around her. By this time, Charles's less reactionary nephew had assumed the throne.

The sound of rustling silk jolted Catherine out of her prayers. Out of nowhere, she saw a form taking shape over the altar. No one else appeared to notice as the Virgin hovered there, wearing a white veil that billowed past her feet, which in turn were poised atop a sparkling sphere.

From where she sat, Catherine gazed astonished at the smaller golden ball that Mary held in her hands. On each finger she wore three rings of different sizes, set with stones. The gems gave off beams of light that poured earthward.

As she sat amid the oblivious crowd, Catherine thought she heard the Virgin saying that the ball between her hands was the world. And the rays of light, Mary said, were graces: free to anyone who asked.

Golden letters began taking shape in the air. Catherine, who had only recently learned to read, struggled to discern the words and commit them to memory: *O Mary, conceived without sin, pray for us who have recourse to thee.*

The image twirled slowly, changing into a wordless insignia including two bleeding hearts and Mary's initial, M.

The service continued all around her as Catherine strained to hear the Virgin's voice. It was telling her to have medals made depicting what she had just seen. Those who wore the medals around their necks would, Catherine heard, receive divine favor.

SHE TOOK HER story to Father Aladel. While he had received her previous revelations frostily and with suspicion, now he was being asked to go out into the city and arrange for a kind of jewelry to be manufactured. Catherine was in no position to do this herself. Aladel wrestled with his feelings. Witnesses would later report hearing heated arguments between Catherine and the priest while they were in the confessional, although at the time no one knew what the two were discussing. Catherine herself later recalled that when Aladel expressed doubts about the medal, she threatened to take her story elsewhere. Seething, he called her a "wasp."

In the summer of 1832 the first 1,500 medals were made. They were an overnight success. Word soon spread that the medals' design had been revealed by Mary herself to a certain nun—but no one knew who. Catherine kept her secret, as did Aladel.

Tens of thousands more were manufactured. Within a few years, wearers around the world were reporting miracles.

But Catherine's role in the saga was over. After that November day, the Virgin appeared only once more, briefly, to say they would never meet again.

While the medal rose to international fame, Catherine remained anonymous. She spent her remaining years caring for indigents and alcoholics in the convent's hospice. In 1876—old by then, and certain she would not live long— Catherine wrote a private account of her experiences. At year's end she died. Her secret was out.

THEY SAY IT is not entirely her visions but her humility, her ability to keep a secret and sidestep certain fame for forty-six years, that largely led to Catherine's canonization in 1947.

Nevertheless, she is credited with restoring the Church's shaky hold on French hearts. The medal came along at a time of widespread anxiety and fear. The revolution had left a generation unsure where to place its faith—unsure that what they felt was faith at all. Set out as a mandate by none other than Mary herself, the medal seemed an implacable beacon. Its message was clear and direct, cutting through what confusion the war had wrought: *Pray for us.* Free of political theories and intellectual subtleties, it was a plea any child could understand. And Mary had promised it would work.

Catherine's adventure launched a spate of alleged Marian apparitions. A few of these—at Lourdes, at Fátima in Portugal, at Medjugorje in Yugoslavia—have become famous worldwide. In those three cases, as in many others, the alleged visionaries are children: not little eggheads, but unworldly young bumpkins. At Fátima as elsewhere, Mary made dire predictions concerning international events: war, peace, the perils of communism. That naïve children bear them only enhances the sense that such messages *must* be divine, mystical and true.

Catherine was no longer a child in 1830. But her near-illiteracy and her status as a country-rube nun gave her a childlike quality. She knew nearly nothing of the world. But as the medals' popularity skyrocketed along with their reputation as ecclesiastical lucky charms, the world would yearn to know about Catherine.

BEATIFICATION PROCEEDINGS BEGAN nearly sixty years after her death. Her body, duly exhumed, is said to have appeared not merely incorrupt but actually still alive: the skin was reportedly soft and creamy-white, the blue eyes open and shining. Treated with chemicals in an effort to preserve its suppleness and color, the corpse was put on display.

Today it lies in the chapel. The marble wall nearby is marked with Mary's monogram as it appears on the medal. The corpse's eyes are indeed wide open, staring up sky-blue with a slickness that would make all but the most devout think: *Glass.* The wimpled head with its almost-cleft chin rests primly on a white satin pillow trimmed in gold cord. With the pious pragmatism with which saints are dismembered, Catherine's actual hands have been amputated and are enshrined elsewhere. Lifelike waxen hands have been attached to the stumps that emerge from her wide sleeves. Black rosary beads are draped around the fingers, joined as if in prayer.

And her heart is gone as well, disengaged and sent to yet another shrine.

ON THE FAR side of the altar lies a glass-windowed casket mounted on dainty golden feet. Dressed in a habit, the life-size waxwork inside contains the bones of St. Louise de Marillac, who co-founded with Vincent de Paul the Sisters of Charity, whose convent this is, in 1634.

After marrying against her will, she made a private vow that if she outlived her husband she would never wed again and would become a nun.

Her husband, Antoine, became ill.

After he died, the widowed Louise put herself under the spiritual direction of a priest she had known for some time: Father Vincent. Together they organized a religious order whose nuns were not cloistered but permitted to go out in public. Ministering to what were literally captive audiences, the nuns focused their efforts on sick men, orphans, and abandoned babies, as well as to galley slaves and prisoners.

IN THE CHAPEL'S foreyard, a chill wind riffles the floral offerings that lie below the bas-reliefs. The clusters of iris and baby's breath, the scattered yellow roses, are still fresh, apparently purchased this morning. Tomorrow they will be gone and a new mass of blooms will replace them.

Rue du Bac is not the Eiffel Tower. Yet, for those who know, it thrives. Ex-voto tablets tile the wall, spanning a century.

Merci a notre mere pour sa protection.
Reconnaissance eternelle a ma mère, succes examen.
Merci ma Bonne Mère—Claude.

Soup Kitchens

▼▼▼▼▼

St. Vincent de Paul
Chapel of the Lazarists
Paris, France

In the October cold, the afternoon sky is white. Tourists stream along the paths at Père Lachaise. A crowd of people gloats, proud of themselves, beside the stone inscribed *Ici Repose Colette*. Yet nearly everyone has the same goal. Scratched into other people's tombs all across the graveyard, defacing those of Paul Dubuffet and Estelle Martin and dozens more is one word, *Jim*. Scratched arrows point the way to Jim Morrison's grave where young visitors from all over the world cluster around snapping photographs and smoking. They shiver under the first spray of rain. The tombstone has a Greek inscription and is scattered with flowers

that have a torn look, as if they were plucked off other bouquets through the cemetery, bloom by bloom.

A frat boy wearing loafers and a V-neck sweater snaps a
picture. "Goodbye, my amigo," he says loudly with a mock
salute. His buttocks will grow big with age, you can tell.

RAIN SWEEPS ALONG the street, sounding like gasps and
soaking a red fez which someone has left outside on a bal-
cony, perhaps by accident. Rain bangs the glass door of a
pharmacy behind which a giant inflatable pill hangs from the
ceiling on a string. The Lazarist church's plain façade is easy
to miss. In fact I walk past it twice while searching for it, first
this way then that as the rain wets my hair and fills my ears
and the red fez slackens behind a grille.

The church saves all its glamour for the inside. Stained-
glass windows glower, garnet, on this sunless day. A deep
blue ceiling, painted with meanders, curves a little like the
sea. The seats are empty, rows of them receding in a silence
all the more resplendent, all the more grotesque, because it is
right in the middle of the city. On the floor, just in the aisle,
a broad-hipped porcelain vase is packed with yellow mums,
as if to make fun of the absent sun.

Above the altar, halfway to the ceiling, is a loft. Burgundy
curtains hang in heavy folds, suspended from an arch, as if
for plays. Before the curtains is a dazzling silver coffin with a
clear glass front.

Angels encrust the coffin, so bright that I squint. One
angel tips a cornucopia, disgorging fruit. Others pose with
their wrists bent back as if in wonder. Silver whorls and
shells and spirals frame the window. Behind this, the relics of
St. Vincent de Paul have been made exquisite. Dressed in
gold brocade and lace, the waxwork looks exactly like a
sleeping man.

But not just any ordinary man—it looks like David Niven dreaming in a treehouse.

Stairs lead from behind the altar to the loft, to give pilgrims a closer look. The glass pane over Vincent's waxwork is a mass of sticky smears and thumbprints, phantom votives. Up close, you can see the large nose with its soft mustache, the lips just faintly pink as if he has been sneaking cherry jam. In certain lights the mouth suggests a smile: the fleeting secrets of a sleeping man. There is a dark dot of beard beneath the lower lip, a fringe over the chin.

Square-toed black shoes with silver buckles rest against the embossed metal wall. Fringed gold brocade lies all along his chest and dangles past his knees. His wide sleeves are white frothy lace, picked in a flower pattern, scalloped at the hem.

I have been here alone for quite some time when a lone pilgrim enters the church and climbs the loft. He wears a hooded navy sweatshirt with a plastic brooch depicting Our Lady of Czestochowa with her staring eyes and wounded cheek.

Below us, in a booth next to the door, the woman selling postcards coughs, a frayed sound like sweaters tearing. Her gooseneck lamp offers the only bright spot there below.

Chapelle sous surveillance electronique, reads a sign.

VINCENT MADE NO secret of the fact that he joined the priesthood dreaming of the easy life that came with it. In 1600, when Vincent was ordained, sharp clerics who found work as aristocrats' personal chaplains were habitually well-rewarded, even with property. Vincent got his wish: appointed chaplain to Queen Marguerite of Valois, he was awarded a small abbey all his own.

In time he was to find yet more work among the rich. As a tutor and chaplain to a landowning family, he made leisurely trips back and forth across his employer's vast estates.

But one of his tasks as the landlord's chaplain was to serve as priest for the man's servants and laborers as well. Leaving the rich man's house on one of these errands, Vincent would find himself in a laborer's hovel, marveling at the contrast.

He took to asking the workers about their lives. Never having been poor himself, he felt his eyes widening with every story he heard. For the lush-living priest, a harsh new world was coming into focus—a world in which God's creatures worked themselves sick. They came home to crowded lodgings where their numerous children, too, were underfed, overlooked, unschooled and given adults' work to do. Vincent could see how these conditions eroded the workers' humanity and their faith.

The more he heard, the more he began to think of those who were even worse off than these laborers. After years of living among the rich, now he could not get the jobless and the homeless out of his mind. He thought of Paris's boulevards as he had last seen them, lined with beggars. He thought of the insane and the ill with no money for doctors. He thought of orphans, and of the increasing number of babies who were placed in baskets by their mothers and abandoned on doorsteps or in alleys forever. In Vincent's time, no social systems looked after any of these groups. No government funding came to their aid, nor any welfare programs, shelters, community centers, or food banks. They were all outsiders, mostly living on the street, and they were on their own.

The more he thought about it, the worse he felt. Waves of shame assailed him as he remembered having lived so comfortably while others were aching, freezing and starving. But then he had an idea. Perhaps he could use his connections with the rich to help the poor. Then, perhaps, his lush living had *not* been such a crime.

At once he began organizing groups of clergy and laypersons who felt as he did. Drawing on funds donated by his
current and former employers and their friends, Vincent
began establishing charitable institutions wherever he could.
He sent members of his groups out into Paris to care for the
sick, to aid prisoners and orphans. With the wealthy widow
and future saint Louise de Marillac, he launched a new religious order called the Sisters of Charity, whose nuns were
committed to such work.

Abandoned children upset Vincent most of all. In Paris,
they were commonplace. Often they were taken in by beggars
who purposely maimed them, hoping such youngsters would
reap sympathy—and alms—from passersby. Foundlings often
died of hunger and neglect. Some who lived were up for sale.

Vincent instructed his female disciples to purchase twelve
foundlings. These twelve became the first residents of his new
institution whose staff comprised nurses and Sisters of
Charity. Within a few years, Vincent's foundling institution
was home to more than three thousand.

Word spread, and aristocrats from all over France were
subsidizing Vincent's new projects. Along with the
foundlings' home, he ran several hospitals. But he also
launched what was then, in the early seventeenth century, a
radically new idea: a workhouse.

Tens of thousands of men and women who had been
sleeping on the streets came to live at this asylum. Here they
were given meals, beds, and menial jobs. Food and tender-
ness did not come absolutely free: a hefty dose of preaching
came with it.

With hindsight, this like most of Vincent's other institutions sends a shudder down the spine. Their very
names—orphanage, asylum, poorhouse, workhouse—inspire
shocking images of Oliver Twist. These are the clumsy,

demoralizing institutions that twentieth-century reformers systematically worked to abolish, replacing them with the programs we know today. Yet Vincent's institutions, when he founded them, were considered outrageously progressive. Vincent has been sainted for his generosity, for giving orphans a home. It was better than nothing.

During the Thirty Years War, Vincent worked to aid France's stricken regions. Tens of thousands of refugees joined the poor who ate daily at the soup kitchens he operated. Vincent's disciples doled out servings of soup that was made according to the priest's own recipes.

War created other dangers besides hunger. The thought of sex-starved soldiers roving the provinces worried Vincent. He made arrangements so that hundreds of girls were brought from the countryside and given shelter in Paris.

He set his sights beyond France's borders. It was a common practice among North African pirates to seize European travelers and sell them into slavery. In Vincent's time, as many as tens of thousands of Christians were living as slaves. In 1645, he sent disciples to the region, where they worked to ransom as many as they could. Perhaps it is through this connection that a legendary tale later arose, which was eventually disproven, in which Vincent himself was briefly enslaved in Tunisia.

Vincent died an old man in Paris, adored as a champion for the poor. Nearly eighty years later, he was canonized. His body was exhumed and witnesses noted that only its eyes and nose were decayed. Later it was exhumed again, and seepage had decomposed the flesh.

In 1833, a twenty-one-year-old Parisian student named Frederic Ozanam—he was named a saint himself in 1997—created the Society of St. Vincent de Paul. Now thriving in over 125 countries around the world, the society's tens of thousands of chapters operate thrift stores and solicit donations for the poor, distributing goods, cash, food, and a Christian message.

LIKE CHINA'S CULTURAL Revolution nearly 200 years later, the French Revolution took aim at religion. Secular heroes overthrew saints. Taboos were shattered as revolutionaries dashed into churches and broke or burned what they could. Of the relics that once enchanted medieval Europe, many were lost forever during the revolution.

French clerics scrambled to secure what they could. Vincent's corpse, just over a hundred years dead, was taken to the first of its many hiding places. Not until 1830 was the coast considered clear enough to bring it back into the open. Amid days of celebration, the silver casket was installed in the Lazarist church on rue de Sevres. Inside, Vincent's relics were ensconced in an exquisite waxwork that had been crafted to duplicate his appearance as closely as possible.

It was scarcely a hundred years later, during the Nazi occupation, when the relics were taken into hiding again. After the war, they were brought out once more.

TODAY THE WAXWORK, with its musing half-smile, overlooks the silent church. One stained-glass window depicts Vincent as a boy, his halo like a poker chip.

Not far from the door is a wooden carving of a corpse wearing a Chinese robe and hanging, strangled, from a post. A plaited queue hangs past the corpse's waist. A Chinese name is chiseled on the statue's base.

The man is not Chinese.

A full beard swells below a pointed nose and closed Caucasian eyes.

In a marble tomb below, adorned with brass bamboo, lie

the relics of St. Jean-Gabriel Perboyre. A French missionary devoted to Vincent de Paul, he sailed for Asia in 1835. Reaching Macao, he continued in a junk to China proper. Jean-Gabriel began walking across the countryside. For eight months he traveled on foot, covering nearly 4,000 miles before he reached Hunan, which had a Christian mission.

Times had changed in the 300 years since Francis Xavier died in despair while trying to enter a China from which Europeans were banned. Europeans were admitted now, though not widely liked. Nor were they much trusted—as Francis Xavier would have done, they brought their foreign religion and tried to make the Chinese believe in it. Some local authorities took particular umbrage at this.

Jean-Gabriel was arrested. Held in a Wuhan jail, he was able to send out a letter telling how he had been interrogated dozens of times, and tortured.

"I remained for half a day kneeling on chains," the priest wrote. "I was given 110 strokes with the bamboo because I did not want to tread on the cross." Of the twenty Christians who were imprisoned and tortured alongside him, Jean-Gabriel writes, "two-thirds publicly renounced their faith."

In the fall of 1840 he was executed. Now his shrine creates a small unexpected spot of exoticism on this rainy Paris day. Someone has left a pot of tiger lilies for Jean-Gabriel, real ones, their pistils trembling as I breathe on them.

MEANWHILE, HIGH ABOVE this, Vincent dreams.

Cousins

▼▼▼▼

St. Knud Lavard
Church of St. Bendt
Ringsted, Denmark

On the train, a group of beautiful young men is playing cards, a boyish game with lots of shouting. Danish sounds like English, tangled, in a dream. They are eating gumdrops, sugar-spangled pulp tinting their teeth. They laugh and shout against a darkening sea sky.

The Danish flag flutters from poles in backyards, any day, not just on holidays. It is a simple flag, an urgent one, the red and white of fire and ice, of blood and bone.

I arrive in Ringsted late on a Saturday afternoon after the banks have closed. They will stay closed all Sunday too and

I have what amounts to four dollars in Danish *kroner*. My landlady, who rents out her basement, says she will accept payment on Monday. The problem is how to stay alive that long. This is an expensive country. My landlady has not offered any food and it is apparent by the way she shuts her refrigerator door that she is not going to. The town has two banks. One has a dysfunctional ATM and the other has no ATM at all. All the markets, with their big signs advertising sales on products which my little dictionary identifies as herring and kale, will be closed until Monday. The town's two restaurants are open, but the meals start at fifteen dollars and I would be ashamed to sit in a roomful of Danes and order, say, a beet. Instead I walk very slowly through the residential district picking wizened fruit off trees. Summer is over and the speckled apples look aborted.

A MAN WAS murdered in 1131 in the woods near here, just outside town. He was a king's son—Erik the Good's second boy, Knud Lavard. His uncle, too, was a king. The uncle raided Yorkshire in 1075 and ended up a saint.

Yet another uncle would ascend to the throne in Erik's wake. This new King Nils was a pagan Norseman of the old school, who felt that his country was unlike others and needed no alliances with others and ought to be proud of that. Fresh in his mind were the Viking ships that had brought Denmark so much wealth from overseas. He loved the gods he'd always known.

Young Knud, having been bypassed for the throne, was Christian. Unlike Nils, he longed to bring Denmark out of its isolation. He envisioned allegiances with Christian lands like Germany, where he had spent some of his childhood, and Russia. He had married a Russian princess. Enchanted with the chivalry he had discovered while living abroad, Knud yearned to institute its arts—along with other foreign concepts—in Denmark.

Now while Nils reigned, Knud was named duke of southern Jutland. He applied himself to seizing and punishing pirates, as well as pressing his religion on whomever he could. His zeal won him a certain admiration among his constituents.

This worried his uncle, the king. Nils had hoped that when his own reign ended, his own son Magnus would naturally take the throne. But Magnus was a youth of no distinction. Knud's popularity menaced his cousin's chances at kingship. As Nils and Magnus watched him from the royal house at Haraldsted, a few miles north of Ringsted, they seethed.

While on a visit, Knud was ambushed and murdered in the Haraldsted forest. Heading the plot were his own cousin Magnus and the king.

KNUD'S MURDER LAUNCHED a civil war. For long years, rivals fought over the kingship. Magnus was never to snare the throne. In 1157, Knud's son Valdemar was crowned absolute sovereign.

Born to his Russian princess mother a week after his father's murder, Valdemar inherited Knud's faith. Under his rule the old gods of sky and sea would breathe their last. Throughout Denmark, pagan sanctuaries were sacked. Their idols were decimated for firewood.

Valdemar erected a royal church in Ringsted to house his father's remains. Yet it didn't seem enough. He asked the pope to declare Knud a saint. By 1169 it was done.

It had been a political killing. As a favor for a king, it was also a political sainting.

TODAY THE CHURCH of St. Bendt, Valdemar's church, surges fortresslike from the green lawn of a city park where

Danes are strolling in the afternoon light smoking pipes and watching their grandchildren kick around a ball with a picture of a duck on it. As if to remind us all of Denmark's bloody heritage, the church's dense reddish brick, laid by Italian artisans far from home, is the color and texture of scabs. Built over the remains of an older church, it became a favorite with pilgrims soon after Knud's relics were entombed there in 1170. Rumors of miracles arose.

For nearly two hundred years, throughout most of the Middle Ages, Danish kings and queens were buried here. A Benedictine monastery once flanked it to the south and west. But the monastery is long gone, burned down in 1806. And the monks who dwelt here and whose music filled this church sing no more. Knud and Valdemar overthrew their country's old religion, only to have a still-newer religion overthrow theirs, centuries hence. Today the church of St. Bendt, like Denmark itself, is Protestant.

YET, INSIDE, IT looks pagan. Jagged pentagrams and bold mandalas mark the tufa walls, its ceiling beige and white with well-placed bits of blue just like the shore. The floor is dark stone slabs, the woodwork unpolished and pale as sand. A hundred royal coats of arms march down the walls, depicting fairy tale birds and beasts. These are not the soft lustrous tassel-tailed lions of Renaissance churches, but flat spiky creatures whose claws are as big as their heads and whose penises jut out like knives.

The coats of arms depict a severed arm clutching a club; a brown chipmunk; a unicorn.

Along with pews, the church has Danish-modern chairs whose seats and backs are plaited straw. It keeps its silence.

Still, its frescoes show who's boss—at least, who *was*. The Virgin holds the Christ child while a female saint holding a frond proclaims her martyrdom. They have the tiny heads and massive bodies of medieval art. Still more show kings and queens all richly crowned. Knud, haloed, holds a feudal flag. King Erik Plovpenning, a later royal martyr, is shown being decapitated and thrown off a boat. A certain Queen Dagmar prays.

Valdemar's tomb is topped with a black stone and the chiseled Danish words that mean *Here lies King Valdemar I, holy Knud's son.*

In a glass case are hanks of hair cut from a queen and a king, and the plaster cast of one queen's skull. But the tomb that once held Knud Lavard's relics is mostly empty now. Just a few token bits of him remain. Shortly before the Reformation, St. Bendt's Benedictines spirited the bulk of Knud's body to France, where it was thought they would be safer from rampaging Protestants. They were right, in a way.

Carved graffiti in the choirstalls read *Hans Christensen 1779*, and *Diderich Kokansky Anno 1730.*

The caretaker explains how just a smidgen of Knud's relics lie under his grave marker, under the floor. He points out features of the church that played various roles in Catholic masses.

"But," says the red-haired man, waving his hands as if tracing the arc of something dissolving in midair, "we don't use the church that way anymore."

A CANDY STORE has opened for the evening. Big gleaming plastic bins are filled with chocolate disks, coconut squares and caramels. Hollow pipes of licorice stuffed with yellow filling, pink, white, green. Gluey candies crafted to look like fried eggs. Stimorol. Marzipan pigs.

In the strained golden light the foil wrappers shimmer softly. I am wild with hunger. I have finished all the tiny apples and a single plum I climbed a fence to pick.

The rear wall of the store is lined with shelves containing pornographic magazines and videos. Their covers show men wearing zippered leather masks, and naked women with their legs up in the air.

A motorcycle roars to a stop in front of the store and a man wearing a black leather jackets hops off. He rushes in and buys pack of cigarettes as well as a licorice spiral with a sugar daisy in its center.

I ask the candy man where to buy actual food.

He frowns behind the counter with the kind of spectacles that make his eyes look large. He is the saddest candy man I've ever seen.

"The gas station sells food," he sighs like someone mourning, as if everybody knows.

THE GAS STATION has jars of puréed meat, and cans of sausages, and jars of fish rolled tight around themselves, caught in clear gelatin. With the last of my money I buy two cans of tomatoes and a roll.

Drawn and Quartered

▼▼▼▼▼

St. John Southworth
Westminster Cathedral
London, England

i

IT IS THE coldest October anyone can remember in London. So the Cancer Society thrift shop has sold nearly every last sweater.

"We took them all out of the back room this morning and now they're near gone," says a volunteer.

"We're down to bits and pieces, aren't we."

She has scars that pull her features together tightly on one side like a drawstring. It appears difficult for her to speak but she continues gamely as a co-worker fluffs up some crocheted hats. In the far corner of the shop a red-haired man is trying on a crimson cardigan.

"Oh a redhead ought to wear green oughtn't he," says the scarred woman. "But we're all out of those aren't we."

"Go on and look at yourself," says the other. "It's smashing."

"Oh, he's shy."

"Don't be shy, flower, look at yourself. No one will think you're vain."

"You see? Looks lovely. Doesn't matter that it came off the women's rack not the men's. No one's going to tell."

SOMEONE HAS SCRAPED away the last three letters of the decal on a window in the bus to the cathedral. It now says *In emergency, break glass with ham.*

WHITE CANDLES ARE burning in Westminster Cathedral, making it smell like Halloween. Not to be confused with the Church of England's nearby Westminster *Abbey*, the cathedral is Britain's Catholic headquarters, built near the turn of the century over a former prison. Inside, the church is vast and draughty. Its nave is the broadest in Britain. A rough undecorated ceiling evokes the night sky, from which hang odd silvery chandeliers that resemble artillery. A hundred varieties of marble lining the walls gleam as smooth and rich as pastry icing. Mosaics flash in candlelight, speckled with gold that somehow only enhances the cold. The cathedral's fourteen Stations of the Cross were sculpted by Eric Gill, a Briton also known for his erotic art.

ST. JOHN SOUTHWORTH was torn to shreds in 1654. From London, his corpse was taken abroad for safekeeping. But then it was lost.

Now the corpse lies again in John's native England, in the

city where John was drawn and quartered. It wears red velvet vestments with strips of white and with voluminous lace sleeves. The casket's glass roof is slanted like a ski chalet's.

The saint's black-slippered feet touch the far wall of the casket. His arms rest at his sides, like those of a man gazing up at clouds. His amputated hands have been replaced with silver ones. Silver, too, is the face with its prominent cheekbones and mustache. Wearing a soft black hat, the gleaming head tilts dreamily to one side on its red-and-gold pillow. Candlelight catches the delicate arch of the nose, the nostrils like elegant commas.

A woman in a heavy woolen coat strides across the vastness of the cold cathedral, removing her plaid woolen hat and folding it into her pocket. Her leatherette loafers, which squeak on the black and white floor, are flesh tone, so that from a distance she appears to be walking on bare feet. Stepping up into the dark recess that is John's chapel she kneels. She strokes the glass over his body, then pats her head with the hand that touched the glass. Rising, she lights two votive candles ceremoniously, then leaves without paying for them.

It is rush hour, and now commuters are filing into the church shivering and make their way to the pews for a moment of contemplation before going home to their microwaveable pork pies and Victoria sponge. Men's suits swish as they pass me clutching briefcases and, under their arms, folded newspapers whose headlines say *Josie Describes Her Mother's Murder*.

TWO CHURCH WORKERS are manning the church's information booth.

"John Southworth was born in Lancashire in 1592," says the wiry gray-haired one eagerly.

"He was martyred in 1654," the tall nearly bald one interjects.

"But in between," says the wiry one. "But in between—"

JOHN WAS BORN at Blackburn, Lancashire, like in the Beatles song. After becoming a priest in France, he was sent home in 1619 to serve in England. But anti-Catholic sentiment was rife. Henry VIII had launched the Act of Supremacy in 1534, by which the king of England also became head of the Anglican Church. In the years that followed, monasteries throughout the country were disassembled, their memberships dissolved and their properties sold off. Priests and other Catholics were accused of plotting assassinations. New laws arose to keep Catholics from practicing their religion altogether.

John was arrested in 1627 and condemned to death. He waited for his execution first in a castle and then in London's Clink, the grim prison whose very name is now slang for "jail." Poised on the Thames, the dank prison was outfitted with a full array of torture devices. But John was lucky—this time. Along with more than a dozen other priests, he was released from the Clink in the spring of 1630.

He went back to the evangelizing which he loved and for which he knew he might very well die. In London's seedy Westminster district—where the cathedral stands today—John was well-known. He sought out plague victims and lingered in their homes, attempting to convert them as they died. Arrested again in 1637, John found himself back in the Clink. The following summer he was released, only to continue evangelizing so diligently that he was arrested yet again that December.

He stood trial at the Old Bailey. Charged with the crime of being a Catholic priest, John pleaded guilty. Now for the second time in his life John found himself facing a death sentence.

He professed his faith from the gallows.

The method of execution most commonly used on condemned Catholics in that era was to hang the victims by their necks until just before they lost consciousness. The noose was removed as the victims, still alive, were cut open and made to watch while their intestines were pulled—"drawn"—out of their bodies. Then the exposed viscera were torched, and often the victims were also beheaded, before their bodies were cut or torn into pieces—"quartered."

Huge crowds watched as, on a late June day in 1654, John was taken from the gallows, then drawn and quartered.

OF THE MANY Catholics executed under English law during the sixteenth and seventeenth centuries, forty were selected and canonized in 1970. Called the Forty Martyrs of England, they were allotted a collective feast day, October 25—just as St. Ursula's eleven thousand virgins and Herod's Holy Innocents also celebrate joint feast days.

John Southworth is one of those forty.

"HE'S OUR OWN martyr," says the bald man in the cathedral, pointing at the floor to denote the Westminster district.

"After working so hard in what was then a very slummy area," says the wiry one, his finger trailing back and forth as if we could see through the walls to the neighborhood beyond, "he was arrested."

"The man who informed on him," the bald one begins hotly, as if at a dinner party describing an upsetting event that had taken place the preceding day, "was the subcurate."

"The lowest of the low."

"It was said the judge at Southworth's trial had tears streaming down his face."

"So Southworth was the last priest to be martyred under Cromwell."

"Last except for what's-his-name."

The name escapes them, and I do not wish to press.

John's execution was held at Tyburn, which is now London's Marble Arch.

"I walked there last summer because I wanted to see the actual place," says the bald one, swinging his arms to mimic hiking. "I thought at the time it was right under the archway but no, it wasn't."

"At the top of Edgware Road is a little traffic island you can see," his friend puts in, "where the Tyburn tree was. There's a chapel not far away."

THE SPANISH AMBASSADOR was among the crowd watching John's execution. It is said that he purchased the torn and bloody body. The Duke of Norfolk's family aided in this process. Two years later, a son of the Earl of Arundel credited John's relics with a miracle cure.

The corpse was taken across the channel to Douai in France, where John had studied and been ordained. There it was laid to rest, and John's grave began to lure pilgrims. During the French Revolution, it was removed, hidden only to become lost for well over a hundred years.

Treasure-seekers poking metal sticks into the ground are said to have happened upon it. Inside were human remains "which were cut into four quarters so they had to be John's," crows the bald one. Allegedly the corpse was missing its hands but the head still had its brownish mustache. The relics were duly returned to England and placed in Westminster Cathedral in 1930.

When Pope Paul VI canonized John along with the other Forty Martyrs, "there was a big ceremony in Rome, wasn't

there," recalls the wiry one. Westminster Cathedral's choir
went and sang in Rome.

A LACE FRILL hides John's ankles.

Having been through so much, this body is smaller than a
normal man's. The silver hands are half the size of mine. The
whole sad story makes me want to pick the little body up and
bundle it between my arms.

I do not, at first, notice the boy wearing a knapsack who
has entered the chapel. Dark hair falling spikily across his pale
forehead, he sits down beside me in a darkness broken only by
the two votive candles. His American accent startles me.

"Excuse me," he says, pointing to the casket. "Who is this?"

Which is jarring because, during all these months of traveling, no one has ever spoken to me in a church. Not like
that, out of the blue.

I tell him as well as possible about John. The knapsack and
sweatshirt and sneakers make me wonder which American
college it is whose fall semester he is at this moment skipping.

"I've heard there is another of these, somewhere," he says,
staring at John. The light catches a fine down on his chin.
"A girl."

"But there are lots of them," I say.

I ask him if he's Catholic and he says he is.

"But still I've never seen something like this."

Candlelight pulses on John's silver face, its silver eyes
wide open.

"I've heard some of them never rot." The boy crosses his
legs, uncrosses them.

"Yeah, well." I shrug and watch his eyes. "They say it is
a miracle."

Selected Bibliography

▼▼▼▼

Attwater, Donald. *A Dictionary of Saints*. New York: Penguin Books, 1965.

Baring-Gould, the Rev. Sabine. *The Lives of the Saints*. Edinburgh: John Grant, 1914.

Caxton, William. *The Golden Legend*. London: J. M. Dent & Co., 1900.

Cruz, Joan Carroll. *The Incorruptibles*. Rockford, IL: Tan Books, 1977.

————. *Relics*. Huntington, IN: Our Sunday Visitor, Inc., 1984.

Di Donato, Pietro. *The Penitent*. New York: Popular Library, 1962.

Di Mercurio, Sister Marie. *Angela*. St. Martin, OH: The Ursulines of Brown County, 1970.

Drane, Augusta Theodosia. *The History of St. Catherine of Siena*. London: Burns & Oates, 1880.

Englebert, Omer. *Catherine Labouré and the Modern Apparitions of Our Lady*. New York: P. J. Kennedy & Sons, 1958.

Frazer, Sir James George. *The Golden Bough*. New York: Macmillan, 1927.

Kinder, Hermann and Hilgemann, Werner. *The Anchor Atlas of World History*, Vol. 1. New York: Anchor Books, 1974.

Lambourne, Paul Higgins. *Pilgrimages*. Englewood Cliffs, NJ: Prentice-Hall, 1984.

Selected Bibliography

▼▼▼▼▼

Madden, Daniel. *A Religious Guide to Europe*. New York: Macmillan, 1975.

Maynard, Theodore. *The Odyssey of Francis Xavier*. London: Longmans, Green & Co., 1936.

Proserpio, the Right Rev. Dr. Leo. *St. Gemma Galgani*. Milwaukee: Bruce Publishing Co., 1940.

Türks, Paul. *Philip Neri, the Fire of Joy*. Edinburgh: T & T Clark, 1995.

Williams, Caroline. *Saints: Their Cults and Origins*. New York: St. Martin's Press, 1980.

Yeo, Margaret. *A Prince of Pastors: St. Carlo Borromeo*. London: Longmans, Green & Co., 1938.